INSIDE IRAN

INSIDE IRAN

THE REAL HISTORY AND POLITICS OF THE ISLAMIC REPUBLIC OF IRAN

MEDEA BENJAMIN

O/R

OR Books

New York · London

Library of Congress Cataloging-in-Publication Data: A catalog record for this book is available from the Library of Congress.

British Library Cataloging in Publication Data: A catalog record for this book is available from the British Library.

Typeset by Lapiz Digital, Chennai, India.

paperback ISBN 978-194486-965-6 • ebook ISBN 978-194486-966-3

TABLE OF CONTENTS

Map: Joe Perez/Poco Meloso

INTRODUCTION

My first trip to Iran was in 2008. I was traveling with my CODEPINK colleagues Jodie Evans and Ann Wright, and trip organizer Leila Zand. It was just after President Obama's historic election, and we were excited about the possibilities of improving U.S.-Iranian ties, even though Iran was still governed by conservative President Ahmadinejad. We considered ourselves citizen diplomats, modeling the kind of outreach we wanted to see in the new administration.

I must admit that I was apprehensive about traveling to Iran as an American Jew, since for decades the Iranian government has had hostile relations with the United States and Israel. On our very first day, we passed a building with a banner that read "Death to America; Death to Israel." Habib Ahmadzadeh, an Iranian filmmaker who was showing us around, laughed. "Don't take the slogans literally—or personally," he said. "They're meant to show opposition to government policies, not people. You'll find that Iranians love Americans." Indeed, all the Iranians we met expressed admiration for Americans, even though U.S. economic sanctions were making their lives so difficult.

What surprised me even more was their admiration for Jews. "We don't like the policies of the Israeli government, but we love Jews," I was told over and over again. Secular Iranians talked glowingly about Jewish creativity in Hollywood and business. Conservative Muslims said we have the same God, many of the same prophets, and are both are descendants from Abraham. A 2014 poll conducted by the US Anti-Defamation League left the pollsters stunned: It found that the most pro-Jewish people in the Middle East, aside from Israelis, were Iranians.

During this visit we met with all kinds of people, both publicly and privately. We met government officials, as well as people who had been imprisoned by the government. We met religious and secular folks, environmentalists, women's groups, and businesspeople. We had chance meetings with people on the street who invited us into their homes. We were overwhelmed by the world-renowned Iranian hospitality, where a guest is considered a gift from heaven. We were showered with copious amounts of delicious food, endless cups of sweet tea, and more gifts than we could fit in our suitcases.

Iranians, we learned, revere their Persian heritage and culture; they want you to know that they are not Arabs.[1] They speak Farsi, not Arabic, and can recite centuries-old poems by the revered poets Hafez and Rumi. They recall Persian philosophers, artists, and scientists who go back to 500 B.C. They describe in vivid detail how their country has been invaded by Greeks, Arabs, Mongols, British, and Russians, but prevailed with their culture intact. Yes, they are Muslims, and overwhelmingly Shia Muslims, but they celebrate ancient Zoroastrian holidays—to the dismay of conservative clerics. The nation's 2,500-year history shines through in their breathtaking architecture, universally acclaimed literature, and deeply spiritual music.

Since 1979, however, the Islamic revolution has turned the nation into a more sober and isolated society where religious leaders dictate everything from what women must wear in public to who can run for office. It also put U.S.-Iranian government relations on a collision course, starting with a hostage crisis at the U.S. Embassy in Tehran that turned into a 444-day diplomatic standoff.

In more recent times, Iran's nuclear program became a flash point for U.S.-Iranian relations. The U.S., along with Britain,

France, Germany, Russia, and China, spent years negotiating a compromise. An historic breakthrough came in 2015 with the signing of the Iran nuclear deal, known as the Joint Comprehensive Plan of Action (JCPOA). It was the signature foreign policy achievement of the Obama administration, a tribute to reformist Iranian President Rouhani, and an impressive example of what can be achieved when adversaries talk to each other.

Unfortunately, Donald Trump, from the time he was campaigning for president, called it "the worst deal ever" and vowed to tear it up. His first foreign trip as president was to Iran's nemesis, Saudi Arabia, where he crowed about clinching Saudi arms sales worth $110 billion (most of which were deals already signed under Obama) and denounced Iran as a nation that "spreads destruction and chaos across the region." He subsequently looked for ways to quash the nuclear deal, imposed fresh sanctions, and even included Iran on the list of countries whose residents were banned from entering the United States, despite the fact that not a single Iranian has ever taken part in a terrorist attack on U.S. soil.

Trump's effusive embrace of the Saudi rulers and antagonism towards Iran is not really a departure from what has been standard U.S. policy for the past 40 years. The Iranian government is certainly guilty of many abuses, including gross violations of free speech and assembly, restricting the rights of women, imprisoning dissidents, and executing people for nonviolent offenses. But when juxtaposed with Saudi Arabia, the U.S. ally is far more repressive internally. Iran has flawed national elections; Saudi Arabia doesn't have national elections at all. Iran's women are restricted, but Saudi Arabia is a much more gender-segregated society. The West applauded the 2017 Saudi announcement that it would allow movie theatres (albeit segregated), while Iran has had a thriving film, theater, and music industry for decades.

In terms of foreign policy, Iran has plenty of blood on its hands, from its involvement in overseas attacks that have killed civilians to its military support for Bashar al-Assad in Syria. While not excusing Iran's record, it is, nevertheless, fair to hold it up against the track record of Saudi Arabia. For decades, the Saudi regime has been spreading its extremist Wahhabi beliefs, which form the ideological underpinnings of terrorist groups from Al Qaeda to ISIS. In 2011, it crushed the nonviolent democratic uprising in Bahrain, and in 2015 it started bombing neighboring Yemen so mercilessly that millions were left hungry and displaced. I document these abuses in my book *Kingdom of the Unjust: Behind the US Saudi Connections.*

Of course, U.S. foreign policy is even more blood-stained. It is ironic to hear U.S. officials accuse Iran of "meddling in the region," meaning the Middle East, when Iran is part of the region and it is the United States that has been sending its military to "meddle" in the region, including the 1991 Gulf War, the 2003 invasion of Iraq, and the 2011 overthrow of Qaddafi in Libya.

The U.S. also has a sordid track record of meddling in Iran's internal affairs. It helped orchestrate the overthrow of elected Prime Minister Mossadegh in 1953 and re-installed the brutal and unpopular Shah, paving the way for the Islamic Revolution of 1979.

In one of Senator Bernie Sanders's rare foreign policy talks, he used Iran as an example of how U.S. intervention and the use of U.S. military power has produced unintended consequences that have caused incalculable harm. "What would Iran look like today if their democratic government had not been overthrown?" Senator Sanders asked. "What impact did that American-led coup have on the entire region? What consequences are we still living with today?"[2]

While we don't know what Iran would look like today if the United States had not helped engineer the 1953 coup, we can venture a guess that there would not have been an Islamic Revolution, that Iran would be a more secular society, and that it would not be on a collision course with the United States.

We cannot remake the past, but we can help shape the future if we are well-informed about Iran, a nation our government teaches us to hate and our media talks about in such a perverted fashion.

This primer on Iran is meant to give the public a basic understanding of the country, both domestically and internationally. It starts with a brief history of Iran's long and proud past, setting the scene for the 1979 Islamic Revolution. It then looks at how the new regime cracked down on human rights and religious minorities, and circumscribed the role that women could play in society. It covers the economy, including how decades of western sanctions have affected daily life. In terms of foreign policy, it delves into the tumultuous relationship with the United States and its neighbors in the region. Throughout, I strive to highlight the pushback and heroic efforts by Iranians eager to live in a more open, more democratic society free of outside interference.

*****

My second visit to Iran was in 2014, when I was invited to give several talks about my book *Drone Warfare: Killing by Remote Control*. On the second day, I did an interview on one of the major state-run TV stations. I gave examples of grieving families from Pakistan and Yemen whose loved ones had been callously blown away by U.S. pilots sitting in secure control rooms thousands of miles away. That evening a young man stopped by the hotel and waited several hours until I arrived. "I could tell from the interview what hotel you were in, and I hope you don't mind that I stopped by," he said in broken English, as he handed me a beautifully wrapped box of chocolates. "I just wanted to thank you for your compassionate stance on behalf of innocent people who have been hurt by your government's actions."

The next day another man stopped by. He was a medical doctor, and he wanted to run an idea by me. "I have been troubled by all the suffering in the world, and also by the dreadful relations between our countries. I would love to see a group of Iranian and American doctors participate in joint humanitarian missions to help people in poor countries like Haiti or Bangladesh. We could show the world how we, the citizens, can work together to help others—no matter what our governments are doing." I loved the idea and took it to medical groups like Physicians for Social Responsibility and Doctors Without Borders, but couldn't find any group to take it on.

There is a deep longing among the Iranian people for close ties between Iran and the West, for moving beyond the divisions our governments create. In a more rational world, Iran and the United States would have full diplomatic relations. Trade with this nation of 80 million pent-up consumers would be a boon to U.S. businesses. Intelligence-sharing and other forms of cooperation would help ensure the defeat of terrorist groups like ISIS. And greater international interactions would strengthen those inside Iran who are advocating for a more open society, and those of us in the United States who are trying to stop our government from dragging us into another bloody conflict.

I hope that this book, designed to give readers a better understanding of the history and dilemmas facing modern-day Iran, can help ignite more passion and creativity to forge new people-to-people initiatives that model the government relations we want to see—and that can help stop the path toward war.

— *Medea Benjamin*
Washington, D.C.
January 2018

CHAPTER 1: IRAN BEFORE THE 1979 REVOLUTION

In the United States, it seems we only become interested in the historical background of our adversaries when it is too late. Our interest peaks after we have allowed our political leaders to define other countries as enemies, after we have killed millions of their people and left their cities in ruins. Our most recent wars have all replaced the problems that were the pretexts for using military force in the first place with even more intractable ones, fueling a seemingly endless cycle of global violence.

Many Americans now understand that Vietnam's National Liberation Front (or Viet Cong), created in 1960, was exactly what it claimed to be: a national liberation movement born of French colonialism and Japanese military occupation. It was not, as U.S. leaders claimed at the time, the vanguard of a Communist plot to take over the world and destroy the American way of life. Our failure to understand Vietnam, its people, or its history cost 59,000 American lives and probably more than three million Vietnamese, Cambodian, and Laotian lives, mostly civilians.

The antipathy between the United States and Iran is likewise rooted in our ignorance of that nation's rich history.

How many Americans understand that Iran's militant rejection of foreign interference in its affairs is the culmination of two centuries of foreign intervention by the British and Russians, from the 19th century "Great Game" to their joint invasions of Iran during two world wars? How many understand that the United States lost its credibility as an anti-colonial ally of the Iranian people in 1953, when it plotted with the U.K. to overthrow Iran's popular elected government and re-impose a repressive, autocratic monarchy?

As in Vietnam and other CIA playgrounds in the post-World War II world, U.S. and British planning for the coup in Iran included an elaborate propaganda campaign directed against their own citizens to tar Iranian Prime Minister Mohammad Mossadegh, a lifelong champion of democracy and constitutionalism in Iran, as a Communist stooge, and to simplistically define Iran as a Cold War battleground. Mossadegh's real "crime" was his determination to ensure that the Iranian people had the right to develop and benefit from their own oil resources, instead of allowing those resources to be pocketed by the British state-owned company now known as BP.

FROM CYRUS THE GREAT TO THE ARAB INVASION

Unlike most of its neighbors, Iran (traditionally called Persia in English) is not a new country carved out of the ruins of the Ottoman Empire. It is one of the oldest countries in the world, older than any Western power, and it has survived within its present borders or wider ones for 2,500 years.[3]

The empire founded by Cyrus the Great (550-350 B.C.), called the Achaemenid Empire, was the first Persian empire to rule across three continents. It stretched from the Balkans to North Africa and Central Asia, with the seat of power in Persepolis. It was an unprecedented attempt to govern a vast array of ethnic groups based on the principle of equal rights for all, including non-interference in local customs and religions. American historian Will Durant stated, "For the first time in known history, an empire almost as extensive as the United States received an orderly government, a competence of administration, a web of swift communications, a security of movement by men and goods on majestic roads, equaled before our time only by the zenith of Imperial Rome."[4]

Cyrus's successors were less successful, succumbing to various invasions. The next Persian empire was the Sassanid dynasty that ruled Iran and much of the region in the 3rd century. It was the last great Persian empire before the Muslim conquest and the adoption of Islam. Its cultural influence, including architecture, art, writing, and philosophy, extended far beyond the empire's borders to Europe, Africa, China, and India. By the 7th century, it had become exhausted by decades of warfare against the Byzantine Empire and succumbed to attacks from Arab Muslims beginning in 633.

The Arabs, inspired by their new Islamic faith, invaded Iran, and, after several decades, managed to replace the ruling Persians. Over time, a majority of Iranians converted to Islam, although many aspects of Persia's unique evolution remained intact, including its language. A synthesis soon evolved between Iran's new Arab rulers and the rich culture of their new subjects. It is said that while Iran was Islamized, it was not Arabized. Persians remained Persian.

Iranian scholars translated the ancient literature of Iran, Syria, and Greece into Arabic, and the House of Wisdom in Baghdad became the greatest library in the world. The works of Plato, Aristotle, Pythagoras, and Archimedes became the basis for new advances in math, science, and philosophy, centuries before they were rediscovered in Europe during the Renaissance.

INVADED BY MONGOLS AND TIMURIDS, PERSIAN CULTURE REMAINS VIBRANT

In the early 13th century, under the leadership of Genghis Khan, the Mongols from East-Central Asia swept into northeastern Iran. They expanded their vast empire, pillaging and burning cities along the way. The Persian people paid dearly for their resistance to the Mongol invasion, losing millions of lives to war and the famine left it its wake.

After the Mongol invasion, a new scourge fell on Iran in 1380: an invasion led by Timur the Lame. Timur had married a Mongol princess and modeled himself on Genghis Khan, razing cities, massacring the people, and building pillars of human heads to commemorate his conquests, which stretched from Moscow to Delhi. Timur was planning the conquest of China when he died in 1405.

The successive ravages by the Mongols and Timurids left Iran much poorer, with agricultural areas turned back to grassland and many peasants returning to lives of nomadic herding. But Persian culture survived, and even the Timurids fell under its spell.

It is clear that although Iran was repeatedly invaded and militarily defeated, it demonstrated a unique resilience. Many of Iran's former enemies, invaders, and foreign rulers were so influenced by their encounters with Iran that they adopted key elements of Iranian language, literature, architecture, and politics.

PERSIA BECOMES A SHIITE NATION

At the end of the 15th century, the Safavids, a religious-based group of Azerbaijani ancestry from northwestern Iran, gained power among the nomadic people displaced by the Mongol and Timurid invasions. The Safavids followed a form of Sufism that blended beliefs from Shi'ism, Sufism, and other pre-Islamic beliefs, based on the millennial teachings of the Sufi mystic Shaykh Safi (1252–1334).

In 1501, the Safavids conquered the northwestern city of Tabriz. Their leader, Esma'il, declared himself *Shah* (King) of Iran and proclaimed Shiism the new denomination. This was the period when Shi'ism became the official religion, and it is often considered the beginning of modern Persian history.

The peak of the Safavid dynasty was the reign of Abbas the Great (1588–1629). The magnificent capital that Shah Abbas built at Isfahan is widely regarded as the crown jewel of Islamic architecture. He expanded trade with both India and Europe, and in 1616, he granted the British East India Company the right to trade in Iran.

Aided by the British, he took back the Strait of Hormuz from Portugal and reestablished Iran's presence in the Persian Gulf. Shah Abbas defeated the Uzbeks in the east and the Ottomans in the West. He moved provincial governors from province to province to prevent them from establishing independent bases of power, and he moved entire communities from one province to another, like the Christian Armenian community he settled in New Julfa, a suburb of Isfahan, whose descendants still live there today.

The Safavid period saw a new flowering of Iranian culture throughout the Muslim world. While the Safavids in Isfahan still spoke their native Turkic language, Farsi became the language of diplomacy and literature. The stability of the Safavid period also allowed the Shiite clergy to establish a powerful role in Iranian society, and there were occasional bouts of persecution of Sunnis, Sufis, Jews, Christians, Zoroastrians, and other religious minorities.

In 1722, the Safavids were defeated by an Afghan army from Kandahar, but that invasion was short-lived. An Iranian warlord named Nader raised a local army, and by 1729, he managed to drive out the invaders and declare himself Shah. With a thirst for conquest, Nader went on to assemble the largest army in the world at that time, about 375,000 troops, invading and conquering lands from India to Iraq. The demands his wars placed on his own people, however, provoked a revolt in Iran, which he put down with great brutality. He was assassinated in 1747 by his own bodyguards.

Nader's death was followed by a period of anarchy, with his former warlords carving out their own fiefdoms. Plagued by war, disease, and emigration, Iran's population fell from nine million to six million.

RUSSIAN, BRITISH, AND FRENCH RIVALRIES PLAY OUT ON IRANIAN SOIL

At the end of the 18th century, Iran was reunited by Agha Mohammad Khan, the leader of the Qajar tribe. He captured Isfahan in 1785, Tehran in 1786, and Shiraz in 1792. He was crowned Shah of Iran in 1796, and Tehran became the capital of his dynasty.

Although the Qajar dynasty maintained its stronghold until the early 20th century, Agha Mohammad Khan did not live to enjoy power for long, as he was assassinated a year after being crowned. He was succeeded by his nephew, Fath Ali Shah, who reigned for 37 years. After the wars and chaos of the 18th century, this was a period of recovery and peace for the Iranian people.

This period, however, also saw the growth of British, French, and Russian influence, as well as intense rivalry among these foreign powers. The British East India Company sent a 500-strong mission to Iran in 1800, and Fath Ali Shah signed a treaty and an arms deal with the British, granting them commercial privileges to the exclusion of the French.

When Russia aggressively annexed the Iranian province of Georgia, Fath Ali Shah asked the British for help. They refused, as they were now allied with Russia against France. The French exploited these differences and signed a treaty with Iran in 1807, agreeing to replace Britain as Iran's European protector and trading partner. But a month later, France made peace with Russia, and the British sent a new mission to win Iran back.

The U.K. and Iran signed a new treaty in 1809, in which the British promised support against any European power that attacked Iran, including Russia. But in 1812, when the British were called upon to arbitrate a new treaty between Russia and Iran over disputed lands of the Caucasus, the British favored Russia. Iran was forced to hand over Baku, Tbilisi, Darband, and Ganja to Russia, and the Iranian Navy was excluded from entering the Caspian Sea. Iranians began to view the British as duplicitous and self-serving allies, a reputation the British have struggled to overcome in their relations with Iran ever since.

Iranians felt like pawns in what became known as the "Great Game," a term used to describe the 19th century confrontation between the British and Russians over territories in Central and South Asia.

Iran's rulers played into this game, making economic deals with these foreign powers to pay back debts they had accumulated, in part because of their extravagant lifestyles. Beginning in the early 1870s, Iranian leaders granted a series of enormous economic concessions to British interests. The first, in 1872, was known as the Reuters Concession. It handed to Baron Julius de Reuter control over the nation's roads, telegraphs, mills, factories, mineral extraction, forests, and public works. British statesman Lord Curzon called it "the most complete and extraordinary surrender of the entire industrial resources of a kingdom into foreign hands that has probably ever been dreamed of."[5] This deplorable deal was scrapped after only one year due to a combination of local outrage and pressure from Russia.

In 1890, another British businessman, Major G.F. Talbot, was granted full control over the production, sale, and export of tobacco for fifty years.[6] Tobacco was a prized, profitable crop, and the industry employed many local workers. The merchants and *ulama* (Shiite clerics) joined forces to push back against the agreement. The tide turned when leading Shia cleric Mirza Hasan Shirazi issued a *fatwa* (religious ruling) banning the use of tobacco, which was widely consumed at the time. By the next month, the Shah was forced to take the concession back from the British. The cleric Shirazi, for his part, then repealed the *fatwa*. This was the period in which the clerics first realized their ability to sway political decisions.

Another regrettable foreign concession, one with monumental consequences, came in 1901, when Iranian rulers signed over the exclusive rights to drill for oil to British businessman William D'Arcy. This move was the first step in what became the U.K. takeover of Iran's oil resources.

The constant duplicity of the foreign governments, together with the deeply exploitive nature of their companies, established a firm belief in the minds of many Iranians that none of these foreign imperialist powers could be trusted. It also fostered growing public frustration at the failure of Iran's rulers to defend the nation's sovereignty.

THE 1906 CONSTITUTIONAL REVOLUTION

The weakness of Iran's central government and the widespread perception that it was corrupted by foreign interests eventually led to the first of Iran's two 20th century revolutions: the Constitutional Revolution, which began in 1905.

MEDEA BENJAMIN

The immediate trigger of the Constitutional Revolution was an economic crisis in 1904–5, caused by the bankruptcy of the government and runaway inflation. The government owed money to foreign powers and tried to collect funds by increasing taxes on bazaar merchants. This led to mass protests by thousands of merchants and students. They presented the Shah with a demand to establish a written constitution and a parliament. On August 5th, a date that is still celebrated as Constitution Day, the Shah signed a proclamation announcing elections for a Constituent Assembly.

A Constituent Assembly was quickly organized, and it oversaw a nationwide election in 1906 for a *Majles* or Parliament (also called the Iranian National Assembly). Although only men could vote (and even they had to be "of higher social status"), this election was nevertheless seen as a breakthrough for a more representative form of government.

The newly elected members of Parliament drafted and approved a constitution based on European models, particularly Belgium's. The Shah remained head of state, but he could only sign laws passed by the Parliament and accept government ministers the Parliament appointed, reducing his role to that of a constitutional monarch, like the heads of royal families in Europe.

The constitution included a bill of rights that gave Iranians the rights of free speech, assembly, and organization; equality before the law; habeas corpus; and protection from arbitrary arrest.

Where this constitution differed from its Western counterparts was in the role of Islam and the Shiite clergy. Shiite Islam was enshrined as Iran's official religion. Only Shiites could hold cabinet positions, and books deemed heretical or anti-religious could be banned. The judiciary was divided between state and *sharia* (religious) courts, and the Parliament could not pass laws deemed to be in conflict with religious law. The Constitution called for the Parliament to elect senior clerics to a Guardian Council to enforce this principle, but this council was never set up until after the 1979 Revolution.

Unfortunately, the first attempt at a representative form of government was short-lived. Several developments strengthened monarchist and reactionary forces, leading to a Civil War that engulfed the nation from 1908 to 1910:

- First, in 1907, the U.K. and Russia signed the Anglo-Russian Convention in which they agreed to divide Iran into British and Russian zones, totally disregarding Iran's national sovereignty. The Parliament was powerless to prevent this, and Iranians learned a hard lesson: the only thing worse than being a pawn in the Great Game between the U.K. and Russia was to confront the two powers working together.

- Second, the parliamentarians soon discovered that tax reform was a hornet's nest of vested interests and traditional privileges that quickly turned many powerful and wealthy Iranians into enemies of the Parliament and the Constitution.

- Third, the liberals stirred up opposition from the clerics by calling for secular reforms on issues like the rights of women and religious minorities. Conservative clerics began to rally huge crowds in opposition.

In June 1908, Mohammad Ali Shah and his supporters, with the encouragement of Russia, staged a military coup against the Parliament, bombarding the building with cannons and killing about 250 people. Six senior members of Parliament were imprisoned; three of them were summarily executed. The coup quickly turned into a civil war when key sectors of Iranian society, from minority groups to Shiite clergy to tribal leaders, took the Constitutional side and opposed the Shah.

When the anti-Shah forces converged in Tehran in 1910, the Shah was forced to abdicate and the Parliament was reconstituted.

More democratic reforms were instituted, including reducing the voting age from 25 to 20 and eliminating status requirements to vote.

The reforms, however, did not resolve an age-old problem: Iran lacked a strong central state capable of collecting revenue. Real power still rested in the hands of the provincial governors and landowners, many of whom had their own private armies and negotiated contracts directly with the British and Russians.

By 1911, the nation was deeply in hock to British and Russian banks. Although the British struck oil in 1908, their first royalty payment to Iran was in 1913—only $15,000, a mere drop in Iran's sea of debt.

When World War I broke out, Iran declared neutrality, but both the British and Russians expanded their occupation of the country. In a brazen display of imperial overreach, the British took advantage of the 1917 Russian revolution to push a scandalous proposal to totally absorb Iran into the British Empire. Britain paid Iran's Prime Minister Vossuq al-Dowleh $600,000 to shepherd this proposal through Parliament, but the entire country rose up against the plan, and the prime minister was forced to resign.

THE RISE OF THE PAHLAVI DYNASTY

In 1921, Reza Khan, a Russian-trained soldier who had risen in the ranks of the Iranian Army, was chosen by the British to lead a brigade to Tehran. Having succeeded in seizing control of the capital, he was initially tasked with heading the army. The ambitious commander, however, wanted more power, and pushed the Parliament to appoint him prime minister. In 1926, the Parliament, dominated by his supporters, crowned him as Shah. Like most Iranians at the time, Reza Khan did not have a surname, and he was informed that he would need a name for his dynasty. This led him to pass a law ordering all Iranians to take a surname; for himself, he chose Pahlavi, the name of the writing system used in ancient Persia.

The Shah succeeded in the task that had stymied every ruler before him: building a strong central state. Using the nation's steadily increasing oil production to provide critical revenues, he created an effective bureaucracy and a large standing army. Although Anglo-Persian Oil paid only a 16 percent royalty on Iran's oil, this nonetheless grew into a tidy sum.

To give Reza Shah his due: he used Iran's oil revenues to build an efficient tax collection and customs system, to build roads across the country, and to invest in new industries. He also built a large, well-equipped military, repressive security services, and new prisons that he filled with thousands of political prisoners. He nearly always wore his military uniform in public, and his government was unapologetically a military regime.

Reza Shah ran a patronage network that made him the richest man in Iran. He reduced the Parliament to a rubber stamp by vetting lists of potential candidates. If the Shah wrote a comment—say, "unpatriotic," "stupid," or "dangerous"—next to a candidate's name, the candidate would be forced to withdraw or end up in prison. Parliamentarians who dared criticize the Shah or his policies fared even worse. Many were killed by death squads or died mysteriously in prison.

The Shah's program of cultural modernization was equally authoritarian. Through military conscription, he forced men to speak Farsi instead of their local dialect and to identify with the state rather than with their own tribe or region. He imposed a national dress code that outlawed tribal and traditional clothes. Men had to wear Western pants, shirts, coats, and the felt-rimmed fedora, or "Pahlavi hat," as it was known. Beards and large mustaches were discouraged.

Women were ordered to remove the *chador* (the traditional dress that covers their bodies and hair, but not their face). The Shah's police would forcibly pull the chadors off women, outraging the Shia clerics and terrorizing women who felt that appearing in public uncovered was tantamount to nakedness.

He called on the international community to change the country's name from Persia to Iran, and to call its citizens Iranians, not Persians.

Reza Shah's government expanded education, but there was little improvement in healthcare, sanitation, or plumbing. Modernization was limited to improvements that would enhance the power of the state and enforce national identity, while things like running water, toilets, and healthcare, which would only improve the lives of its people, were not a priority.

Many of the Shah's measures were consciously designed to break the power of the religious hierarchy. His educational reforms ended the clerics' near monopoly on education, just as the creation of secular courts broke their judicial power. His efforts at Westernization and secularism earned him the enmity of the clerics.

For the most part, the wealthy classes supported or tolerated the Reza Shah regime because they were able to increase their wealth, send their children to universities in Europe, and enjoy the pleasures of modern life. Landowners had the backing of a powerful state to enforce their will on their peasants, and tribal leaders could register formerly common tribal land under their own names, transforming themselves into wealthy, modern landlords.

But Reza Shah was hated by most Iranians, from devout Muslims to exploited working people to educated, middle class Iranians who longed for a democratic state.

In 1934, the Shah signed a new contract with the Anglo-Persian Oil Company, giving it exclusive rights over the nation's oil for the next 60 years in exchange for raising Iran's royalty from 16 percent to 20 percent. This confirmed public suspicion that he was, and had always been, essentially a British puppet.

The Shah was not only negotiating with the British, however. Tired of what he saw as the opportunistic policies of both Britain and the Soviet Union, he sought to counterbalance their influence by encouraging trade with Germany. On the eve of World War II, Germany was Iran's number one trading partner.

Although Reza Shah declared Iran neutral in the war, his ties with Germany backfired when both the Soviets and the British joined forces in 1941 to fight Germany, and decided they needed Iran as a supply route to send war material to the Soviet forces. In August 1941, the British and Soviets both launched a massive air, land, and naval assault against Iran.

The Shah's vaunted army was built to control and oppress his own people, not to resist an invasion. It surrendered after three days. The British gave the stunned Shah a face-saving way out: He could abdicate in favor of his son, Mohammad Reza Pahlavi, if his son would, in turn, allow the British and Soviets to occupy their respective zones in the north and south of the country.

IRAN'S SHORT-LIVED BUT INFLUENTIAL SOCIALIST PARTY: TUDEH

The new Shah, who was only 22 years old, made a show of returning some of his family's ill-gotten land and wealth to the Iranian treasury, ear-marking it to build hospitals, medical colleges, libraries, and a water system. Even as he stressed his Swiss education and Western orientation, he promised the clergy that his government would end his father's Westernization campaign.

The years between 1941 and 1953 marked a brief period of renewed constitutional government, as the Parliament once again became functional. While in the rural areas the majority of seats were controlled by landowners, in the cities a new party began winning over working-class Iranians and young intellectuals: the socialist Tudeh Party. Founded in 1941 by former political prisoners and young graduates of European universities, by 1945 the party held seven seats in the Parliament and three cabinet ministries. Its newspaper *Rahbar* (Leader) had a circulation of 100,000, and about 50,000 people attended its massive rallies in Tehran. The socialist party made significant gains for workers. When the Tudeh-led Central Council of Federated Trade Unions called a strike against the Anglo-Iranian Oil Company in 1946, the company quickly backed down and granted the strikers' demands for an eight-hour day, overtime pay, higher wages, better housing, and even a paid weekly day off for Friday prayers.

The Tudeh Party went on to push through the first national labor law in the Middle East. It granted all workers most of the same rights the oil workers had won. The law outlawed child labor and established minimum wages based on local conditions, six annual holidays, unemployment compensation, and the right to organize unions.

Sadly, it was the actions of the Soviet Union in 1946 that undermined Iran's socialist party. In opposition to Iran's central government, the Soviets supported popular movements for autonomy in Iranian Kurdistan and Azerbaijan. The Iranian government claimed that Tudeh supported the secessionists, and launched a widespread crackdown. The party's previously powerful united front was split between nationalists who opposed the Soviet-backed secessionist movements and pro-Soviet leftists who felt obliged to support them.

The party was outlawed, and its newspapers were shut down. Many Tudeh leaders were arrested; others fled into exile and were sentenced to death *in absentia*. Even opposition politicians who were not Tudeh members were arrested, and the Shah convened a Constituent Assembly to expand his own powers.

The socialist party was banned and suppressed, but it left a lasting imprint on Iranian politics. It had raised the political consciousness of millions of Iranians and issued the first widespread call for the nationalization of the Anglo-Iranian Oil Company, a call that would only ring louder in the years that followed.

MOSSADEGH COMES TO POWER

Into the political vacuum left by the banning of the Tudeh Party stepped Mohammad Mossadegh, a man in his late 60s, from an aristocratic family. He had been a prominent politician during and after the Constitutional Revolution of 1906, but had been forced out of politics by Reza Shah. He was known as an advocate of two principles: strict adherence to the 1906 Constitution and what he called "negative equilibrium," or strict neutrality in foreign affairs to ensure Iran's sovereignty and independence from foreign domination.

Mossadegh contrasted his concept of "negative equilibrium" with Iran's previous practice of "positive equilibrium," by which Iran gave concessions and privileges to Britain and Russia (as well as to Belgium and France), and then tried desperately to find a balance between them as more and more of its sovereignty was eroded.

He denounced past oil concessions granted to the British and Russians, as well as ongoing negotiations with the Americans for new oil concessions. He took up the call to nationalize Iran's oil industry, insisting that it was Iran's inalienable right to have full control over the production, sale, and export of its own resources.

Due to his conflict with the British over oil nationalization, Mossadegh has been portrayed in the West as anti-British, but he was in fact a great admirer of 19th century British liberal democracy. He was simply opposed to handing Iran's sovereignty or its resources over to any other country, whether it was the U.K., the U.S.S.R., or the U.S.

Iranians regarded Mossadegh as incorruptible because, although he was related by blood and marriage to Iran's most aristocratic and wealthy families, he led a middle-class life and denounced the extravagant lifestyles of his fellow aristocrats. After becoming prime minister in 1951, he insisted on being addressed as "Dr. Mossadegh," not as "Your Excellency."

Mossadegh united different parties and social groups to form a coalition called the National Front. He had the support of Ayatollah Kashani, the most politically active member of the clerical hierarchy. The National Front organized petitions and street demonstrations to mobilize a mass movement for the nationalization of the oil industry. In 1951, he introduced his oil nationalization bill in the Parliament and was elected prime minister with a mandate to carry it out.

Mossadegh and his colleagues created the National Iranian Oil Company (NIOC) and began negotiations with Anglo-Iranian Oil Company (the precursor to BP) to hand over its facilities and operations. When Anglo-Iranian rejected the plan outright, he ordered NIOC to take over its wells, pipelines, refinery, and offices throughout the nation. The British government evacuated most of the company's British personnel from Iran and froze Iranian assets in British banks. Mossadegh closed the British Embassy and broke off diplomatic relations.

In 1952, Mossadegh also tried to reform Iran's election laws to weaken the power of the Shah and the wealthiest landlords. When this failed, he halted the parliamentary elections as soon as he had a quorum of deputies who would support him. Then, he provoked a showdown with the Shah by insisting that, as prime minister, he had the right to appoint the war minister as well as all the other members of his cabinet, a prerogative the Shah had always kept for himself. Mossadegh took to the airwaves and told the nation that he needed control of the military to prevent the Shah and the British from undermining his oil nationalization plan. The public flooded the streets for three days of protests against the Shah, who was forced to back down.

Mossadegh made the most of his victory over the Shah. He transferred lands appropriated by the Shah back to the state; prohibited the Shah from communicating directly with foreign embassies; and exiled the Shah's politically active twin sister, Princess Ashraf.

He also tried to get control over the military. He renamed the War Ministry the Ministry of Defense and promised from then on to buy only defensive weapons. He purged 136 military officers and transferred 15,000 men from the army to the police. He cut the military budget by 15 percent, and appointed a parliamentary commission to investigate the Shah's military procurement practices for corruption.

To counteract the pro-Shah members of Parliament, Mossadegh asked his Parliamentary backers to resign, denying the Parliament the quorum needed to overturn his orders. He then called a referendum to ratify his dissolution of the Parliament. By July 1953, a constitutional committee was debating how to replace Iran's monarchy with a democratic republic.

THE 1953 COUP: STAGED BY THE U.K. AND U.S.

The British had a great deal to lose from the nationalization of the Anglo-Iranian Oil Company. The U.K. government earned $92 million in taxes on its operations and $354 million in foreign exchange from oil sales. The British Royal Navy depended on Iran for 85 percent of its fuel.

But, as the British stressed to their U.S. allies, there were larger issues at stake, relating to control of the global oil industry. If Iran succeeded in nationalizing its oil industry, Indonesia, Venezuela, Iraq, and others would surely follow. The Western cartel that controlled the industry would be broken, with dire consequences for both U.K. and U.S. business and geopolitical interests.

In private negotiations, the British were prepared to increase Iran's share of the profits from its oil production from 20 percent up to as much as 60 percent, and to share Iran's oil with other Western companies, but only with the proviso that ultimate control remained in Western hands.

In public, however, the British blamed the crisis entirely on Mossadegh. Historian Ervand Abrahamian compiled a list of the insulting terms they used to smear him: "fanatical," "crazy," "erratic," "eccentric," "slippery," "unbalanced," "demagogic," "absurd," "childish," "tiresome and single-minded," "inflammatory," "volatile and unstable," "sentimentally mystical," "wild," "wily Oriental," "unwilling to face fact," "dictatorial," "xenophobic," "Robespierre-like," "Frankenstein-like," "unprepared to listen to reason and common sense," and "swayed by martyrdom complex."

There was little disagreement between Washington and London about the result they wanted: to keep Iran's oil under Western control. But for fourteen months in 1951 and 1952, the Americans resisted the British line that Mossadegh had to go. U.S. officials tried to negotiate a compromise that would give the Iranians the illusion of nationalization while keeping real control in Western hands. Only after Mossadegh moved against the Shah in July 1952 did the U.S. Ambassador in Tehran make a report to Washington, saying: "Only a *coup d'etat* could save the situation."

The CIA and the U.K. spy agency MI6 began planning the coup in late 1952. MI6 already had an extensive dossier on all of Iran's senior military officers. The Americans had useful assets as well: 100 U.S. advisors embedded in Iran's military, and good contacts with young Iranian officers who had been sent to the United States for training. Those included tank commanders and a clandestine network of unsavory characters in the Tehran bazaars. In June 1953, Secretary of State John Foster Dulles unveiled the plan to policymakers in Washington, announcing, "This is how we get rid of Mossadegh."[7]

On August 15th, the Shah issued a decree dismissing Mossadegh and appointing a new prime minister, General Zahedi, whom the British had imprisoned during the war as a German collaborator. Mossadegh refused to step down and instead broadcast a message that the Shah, encouraged by "foreign elements," had attempted a coup.

The next day, there were huge demonstrations supporting Mossadegh and the National Front, but CIA provocateurs in the crowd attacked clerics and mosques, forcing Mossadegh to condemn the violence. The U.S. Ambassador met with Mossadegh and threatened to evacuate Americans from Iran because of the chaos in the streets. On August 18th, Mossadegh deployed his police and army to suppress the demonstrations.

On August 19th, CIA-paid gangs and soldiers in civilian clothes staged an aggressive pro-Shah, anti-Mossadegh counter-demonstration that brought the turmoil on the streets of Tehran to a climax. Richard Cottam, who was with the CIA in Tehran at the time, wrote later, "The mob that came into north Tehran and was decisive in the overthrow was a mercenary mob. It had no ideology. That mob was paid for by American dollars."[8]

Amid the mayhem, 32 Sherman tanks rolled into the city and surrounded critical buildings, including Mossadegh's home and the main radio station. Three hours later, the coup leaders captured the radio station and broadcast a proclamation from the Shah naming General Zahedi as Iran's new prime minister. Fighting raged on for another six hours between forces backing the coup and troops loyal to Mossadegh. Outgunned, the loyalists surrendered. The *New York Times* estimated that at least 300 people were killed and 100 wounded.[9]

BITTER AFTERMATH OF THE 1953 COUP

President Eisenhower told the American people that the Iranian people had "saved the day," because of their "revulsion against communism," and "their profound love for their monarchy."

In fact, the coup permanently undermined the legitimacy of the monarchy in Iran. It identified the Shah and his military with the imperialist interests of the British and the Americans, and with Anglo-Iranian and the rest of the Western oil cartel that reaped shares of Iran's oil after the coup. Relations between Iran and the United States were permanently damaged, as the U.S. government was now seen as yet another duplicitous power, in cahoots with the perfidious British who had constrained and thwarted Iran's independence and sovereignty for 150 years. By contrast, Mohammad Mossadegh is remembered by his people as a nationalist leader in the mold of India's Gandhi, Indonesia's Sukarno, and Egypt's Nasser.

The crackdown on the National Front that followed the coup was brutal. There were mass arrests, and many of the leaders were executed. Mossadegh spent three years in prison and the rest of his life under house arrest. When he died in 1967, he was buried in his garden to avoid a public funeral that might have ignited a revolution. (Decades later, on the anniversary of his death, thousands of students still gather outside his house and visit his grave to pay tribute to their hero.)

All the secular parties and organizations that had opposed the Shah were dismantled and banned. The only important institution that maintained some independence and could still speak with moral authority to the concerns of the public was the Shiite clergy, setting the stage for the 1979 Islamic Revolution.

MOHAMMAD REZA SHAH RULES WITH AN IRON FIST

Mohammad Reza Shah was back in charge with even more dictatorial powers, ruling much as his father had done. He continued his father's project of building Iran into a strong, centralized, militarized state. Iran was now receiving a 50 percent share of the annual revenue from its ever-increasing oil output, and the Shah poured much of Iran's oil wealth into his first priority: the military. Iran became the largest weapons purchaser in the world, much like Saudi Arabia today. He built the largest navy in the Persian Gulf, the largest air force in the region, and the fifth largest army in the world. The Shah's arsenal eventually included 1,000 tanks, 100 long-range artillery pieces, 400 helicopters, 2,500 Maverick air-to-ground missiles, and 324 U.S.-built warplanes. In 1978, his last year in power, he ordered $12 billion worth of new weapons, including three destroyers, ten nuclear submarines, and another 449 warplanes.

He also built a terrifying 5,000-man security service called SAVAK, which reportedly recruited one out of every 450 adult Iranian men as an informer. SAVAK enforced draconian censorship, and disappeared, tortured, and killed political dissidents.

Frances FitzGerald, who visited Iran as the niece of the U.S. Ambassador, wrote the following in 1974: "Educated Iranians cannot trust anyone beyond a close circle of friends, and for them the effect is the same as if everyone else belonged (to SAVAK). SAVAK intensifies this fear by giving no account of its activities. People disappear in Iran, and their disappearances go unrecorded."[10]

In 1975, Amnesty International estimated that there were between 25,000 and 100,000 political prisoners in the Shah's prisons. Amnesty noted that Iran had "the highest rate of death penalties in the world, no valid system of civilian courts, and a history of torture that is beyond belief."[11]

THE FAILURE OF THE SHAH'S WHITE REVOLUTION

The highlight of the Shah's development program was his 1963 "White Revolution," framed as a counter to a potential socialist "Red Revolution." It was intended to transform Iran into an economic and industrial power, and included new rights for women. The land reform at the heart of the program, however, still left millions in the countryside with no land, or too little land to support themselves. The population of Tehran mushroomed from 1.5 million to more than 5.5 million as landless peasants flocked to shanty towns around the cities to seek work and some scraps from the relative prosperity of city life.

The central structural problem with the White Revolution was that it was based on what we would now call "trickle-down economics." Iran's oil revenues were funneled to the top 0.1 percent of the economic strata, who were part of the Shah's social circle and patronage system, and most of the wealth simply stayed there. This tiny upper class owned 85 percent of the shares in Iranian corporations, sent their children to university in Europe or the United States, and led extravagant, jet-set lifestyles.

Meanwhile, the Shah tightened his political grip. His rubber-stamp Parliament was run by a two-party system, with a permanent majority for the Shah's Iran-e Novin Party and a permanent minority for the token opposition Mardom Party. In 1975, after the opposition won several by-elections by running local candidates not connected to the Shah's patronage system, its leader was killed in a suspicious car accident, and the Shah dissolved both parties. In their place, he created a one-party totalitarian state under his new Resurgence Party. The Shah now condemned multi-party democracy as a sham and declared that his new party would build a perfect society that would be a model for the East and West alike.

Slipping farther and farther into megalomania, the Shah seemed to genuinely believe in a fantasy vision of himself and his country. He told Italian journalist Oriana Fallaci that he was guided by visions and messages from God and from Imam Ali. "I am accompanied by a force that others can't see, my mythical force. I get messages, religious messages."[12]

Inspired by his delusions, the Shah launched politically suicidal attacks on two powerful interest groups: the bazaar merchants and the Shiite clergy. He blamed the country's economic woes on profiteering by bazaar merchants, and unleashed an army of 10,000 inspectors to harass them. SAVAK security forces set up "Guild Courts" that brought charges against 180,000 merchants, handed down 250,000 fines and 8,000 prison terms, and banished 23,000 merchants from their home towns.

The Shah's call for women's rights—the right to vote, to initiate divorce, to travel without a man's permission—was fiercely opposed by the religious establishment. The Shah also challenged the clergy by proclaiming himself a spiritual as well as a political leader. He replaced the Muslim calendar with a new Imperial Calendar dating from the founding of the Persian Empire in 500 B.C. He sent inspectors to audit religious endowments and took control of Tehran University's Theology College and other religious education institutions. A clerical newspaper accused the Shah of trying to "nationalize" religion.

Living increasingly in his own fantasy world, the Shah seemed convinced to the end that his people really loved him. In reality, he never had support from the Western-educated intelligentsia or the urban working class, who had been politicized by the socialist Tudeh Party in the 1940s, backed Mossadegh's National Front in the 1950s, and saw the Shah as an American and British puppet. The abuses of the Shah and his Resurgence Party severed his last links with the conservative middle class of merchants, landlords, and clerics who had traditionally supported the monarchy.

The Pahlavi dynasty had run its course.

CHAPTER 2: THE ISLAMIC REVOLUTION SHOCKS THE WORLD

To Western observers, it may seem incongruous that a country that supported the socialist Tudeh Party in the 1940s and the anti-imperialist National Front in the early 1950s was consumed in the 1970s by an Islamic revolution that brought to power what Western commentators have labelled a fundamentalist theocracy.

As in all revolutions, the forces driving it were committed to transforming the political regime, but they represented a complex combination of nationalism, populism, and religious radicalism.

THE RISE OF AYATOLLAH KHOMEINI

Key in the religious mix was Sayyid Ruhollah Musavi Khomeini, known in the Western world as Ayatollah Khomeini. Khomeini had been a leading scholar of Shia Islam, teaching political philosophy, Islamic history, and ethics at seminaries in the religious cities of Najaf and Qom. During the 1960s process of Westernization pursued by the Reza Shah Pahlavi, Khomeini became an increasingly vocal opponent, accusing the Shah of submission to the United States and Israel. In 1963, he was arrested for preaching inflammatory sermons calling for the overthrow of the Shah. News of his arrest led to major riots, which resulted in the death of many of his supporters. Khomeini was exiled in 1964, first in Turkey, then Iraq, then France.

From exile, he lectured and wrote extensively about his views on governance. He believed that rule by monarchs or elected parliaments claiming to represent the people was un-Islamic. He insisted that those holding government posts should be well versed in *sharia*, the laws of God, and that the system of clerical rule was necessary to prevent injustice, corruption, and oppression by the powerful over the poor. He believed that clerical rule was the only way to protect the people from anti-Islamic influences and meddling by non-Muslim foreign powers.

Tape recordings of Khomeini's sermons and banned copies of his books circulated underground inside Iran, where he developed a devoted following among the young clergy, students, and merchants.

UNTIMELY DEATH OF INFLUENTIAL CLERIC ALI SHARIATI

A less widely known—but equally important—religious figure was Ali Shariati. Had he lived to see the revolution, it might have taken a very different course.

Shariati was the son of a cleric and teacher in the holy city of Mashad. He taught in a village school before continuing his studies in Arabic and French at Mashad University. There, he translated into Farsi and Arabic the biography of Abu Zarr, one of the Prophet Muhammad's lesser-known companions. The book was titled, *Abu Zarr: The God Worshipping Socialist.* Shariati's father had held up Abu Zarr as a model to his son, and Shariati became known to many Iranians as the "Abu Zarr of Iran."

In the early 1960s, Shariati won a scholarship to study at the Sorbonne in France, where he took part in demonstrations supporting anti-colonial struggles in the Congo and Algeria and studied under French academic experts in Islamic mysticism. He translated into Farsi works by Jean-Paul Sartre, Che Guevara, Franz Fanon and a book about the war in Algeria. He also studied Christian Liberation Theology as he grappled with the role of religion in anti-colonial struggles.

Shariati embraced Shiism's traditional rejection of worldly authority, especially of monarchy, and connected it with the 20th century's anti-colonial and anti-capitalist struggles. He believed that the Prophet Muhammad had come to establish not just a new religion, but a permanent revolution that would lead to a classless society. In Shariati's interpretation, Imam Ali opposed the early Caliphs because they were betraying the true meaning of Islam by compromising with worldly power.

Shariati attacked the Shiite clerical hierarchy and its relationship with the landowning classes, insisting that their financial support was inherently corrupting. "The task at hand is nothing less than the total liberation of Islam from the clergy and the propertied classes," he declared.[13]

When Ali Shariati died in exile in the U.K. in 1977 at the young age of 44, many suspected foul play by SAVAK.

Shariati's death just before the revolution deprived Iran of a powerful voice that might have led it in a different direction and balanced the power of Ayatollah Khomeini and the Shiite hierarchy. While Shariati's ideas appealed more to young, religious intellectuals than to conservative clerics, they were firmly rooted in Shiism's long tradition of opposition to corrupt worldly authority. Many of Khomeini's sayings that became the slogans of the revolution could equally have been written by Shariati: "Islam belongs to the oppressed, not to the oppressors;" "Islam originates from the masses, not from the rich;" and "Islam is not the opiate of the masses."

TRIUMPH OF THE ISLAMIC REVOLUTION

When President Jimmy Carter took office in 1977 and announced that promoting human rights was a new priority of U.S. foreign policy, the Shah actually pulled back from some forms of repression, such as secret trials of dissidents in military courts. More Iranians began to speak out openly against his atrocities and his one-party state, and students in Tehran took to the streets in protest.

When a government-controlled newspaper ran a savage smear of the Ayatollah Khomeini in January 1978, accusing him of immorality and being a British agent, seminary students in the holy city Qom took to the street. The students were demanding the return of Khomeini from exile and the reopening of his Fayzieh seminary. They also demanded the release of political prisoners; an end to Iran's subservient relations with Western powers; freedom of the press; an independent judiciary; and the dissolution of the Shah's Resurgence Party.

They marched to the police station, where they were viciously attacked. The number of students killed is disputed, with estimates ranging wildly from 5 to 100, but their martyrdom became a new rallying cry.

The most senior cleric, Ayatollah Shariatmadari, called a general strike on the 40th day after the killings in Qom, launching a series of escalating protests every 40 days. The February strike provoked a bloody military crackdown on protesters in Tabriz, Shariatmadari's hometown. Angry demonstrators responded by attacking property that symbolized either the repressive state, such as police stations, or Western values, such as luxury hotels and movie theaters. The second strike in March led the Shah to cancel a foreign trip and take personal command of his riot police, who shut down the protests by firing at the crowd, killing over 100. The third strike in May included protest marches in 24 towns and cities. In Qom, police raided Ayatollah Shariatmadari's residence and killed theology students who had taken sanctuary there. The opposition put the death toll in the three strikes at 250, while the government claimed only 22 students had been killed.

On August 19th, 1978, an incident that helped change the course of history occurred at the Rex Cinema in the city of Abadan. While hundreds of people were watching a controversial film about drug addiction and poverty called *Gavaznha* (*The Deer*), a group of men barred the doors of the cinema, doused it with gasoline, and set it on fire. Over 400 people were killed. Incensed, the public blamed the police chief, who was the same person who had ordered the police to fire on the protesting seminary students in Qom in January. They believed the regime had targeted the theater to kill political dissidents who had gathered to watch the film.

To this day, there remains controversy over who really set the theatre on fire. Some believe it was not Shah supporters but Khomeini supporters who wanted to create more anger against the Shah. Others believe it was the Marxist group called MEK, with the same goal of building revolutionary outrage among the public.

In any case, the tragedy did build anti-Shah fervor. After a huge funeral, 10,000 people marched through the city chanting, "Burn the Shah" and "The Shah must go."

According to historian Roy Mottahedeh, "Thousands of Iranians who had felt neutral and had until now thought that the struggle was only between the Shah and supporters of religiously conservative mullahs felt that the government might put their own lives on the block to save itself. Suddenly, for hundreds of thousands, the movement was their own business."[14]

The Shah declared martial law and, on September 8th, his troops opened fire on a demonstration in Tehran's Jaleh Square. The number of deaths varied widely, but 84 people were identified by the Martyrs Foundation that was set up later to compensate the families of the Shah's victims. September 8th, 1978, became known as "Black Friday" and was seen as the critical turning point that sealed the Shah's fate.

In the following weeks, a general strike took hold of the whole country and on December 11th, the climax of the Shiite festival of Ashura, the government called off the military and permitted four huge but orderly marches to meet up in Tehran's Shahyad Square (which after the revolution was renamed Azadi Freedom Square).

An estimated two million people converged, chanting, "The Shah must go." Speakers called for the return of Khomeini, the expulsion of Western powers, and social justice for the "deprived masses." Noting the orderly, peaceful character of the demonstration, the *New York Times* noted, "In a way, the opposition has demonstrated that there already is an alternative government."[15] With the old regime collapsing, on January 16, 1979, the Shah fled the country.

Two weeks later, on February 1st, Ayatollah Khomeini returned to Iran after 15 years in exile. The crowd that greeted Khomeini at the airport was estimated at three million. As the *Washington Post* said at the time, "The religious, the lay, the left, the liberals, the right, everyone who was fed up with the Shah used Khomeini as a convenient symbol of a strong man who for years openly opposed the monarchy."[16]

His first port of call was the Behest-e-Zahra Cemetery, where he paid his respects to the Shah's victims. The revolutionary government later claimed that 60,000 Iranians died resisting the Shah's regime from 1963 until the Revolution, although the Martyrs Foundation was only able to identify about 3,000, mostly killed between 1977 and 1979, and mainly from working-class districts of Tehran.

On February 9th, revolutionary forces broke into armories in Tehran and surrounded the air force headquarters. The chiefs of staff declared the military neutral and confined the troops to their barracks. The French newspaper *Le Monde* compared the scene in the streets of Tehran to the Paris Commune, with thousands of civilians carrying machine guns and other weapons.

On the afternoon of February 11th, Radio Tehran broadcast the historic message: "This is the voice of Iran, the voice of true Iran, the voice of the Islamic Revolution."

KHOMEINI'S VISION PREVAILS OVER CALLS FOR SEPARATION OF CHURCH AND STATE

An Interim Government was set up and charged with drawing up a new constitution. Mehdi Bazargan, an ally of Mohammad Mossadegh and founder of the Iran Liberation Movement in 1961, was named prime minister. Bazargan was a French-educated engineer. He was a devout Shia Muslim, and his Liberation Movement was not as secular as Mossadegh's National Front, but he firmly supported the separation of church and state. Bazargan drafted a new constitution based on the constitution of France's Fifth Republic.

By this point, however, the real power lay with Ayatollah Khomeini and his followers. They had set up a Revolutionary Council and a Central Committee, and they controlled many of the local revolutionary committees that sprang up at mosques around the country.

The sharpest disagreement between Bazargan and Khomeini was over Khomeini's insistence on including the positions of Supreme Leader and Guardian Council, which is a body that was called for in the 1906 Constitution but had never been established. The traditional "guardianship" role of the Shiite clergy was to oversee religious foundations and protect the weakest members of society, especially children, widows, and the mentally ill. Khomeini reinterpreted this guardianship, or *velayat-e faqeh*, to cover society at large. He wanted to ensure that all government laws conformed to the tenets of Islam, extending religious jurisprudence to allow direct clerical rule of society.

The first consequential test of wills between Bazargan and Khomeini was over the April 1979 referendum giving voters the choice of whether or not they wanted to establish an Islamic Republic. Bazargan argued for giving the public a third choice: to vote for a "Democratic Islamic Republic." Khomeini insisted on an up or down vote for an Islamic Republic, arguing that a true Islamic Republic would be perfect and required no qualification based on Western concepts like "democracy." Khomeini won the argument and with a massive 95 percent turnout, an extraordinary 99 percent of the public voted for an Islamic Republic.

Khomeini's supporters likewise dominated the election for a 73-man "Assembly of Experts" to draft the new constitution. The constitution that emerged retained some democratic elements advocated by Bazargan, including direct elections for the president, a 270-member *Majles* (Parliament), and provincial and local councils. But it gave unprecedented authority to Khomeini as the Supreme Leader (and whoever followed him in that role), and tremendous power to the Guardian Council.

The constitution guaranteed civil liberties, from habeas corpus to the presumption of innocence to freedom of religion, speech, assembly, and the press; and freedom from arbitrary arrest, torture, police surveillance, and wiretapping. It met many of the social demands of the working class and the secular opposition to the Shah. It guaranteed old-age pensions, free primary and secondary education, unemployment compensation, disability pay, decent housing, and universal healthcare. It enshrined even loftier goals like eliminating poverty, unemployment, usury, vice, private monopolies, and inequality—even between men and women. It also called for helping the oppressed of the world in their struggles against their oppressors.

The way in which all these rights and promises were to be implemented, however, had to "conform to the principles of Islam," as determined by the Guardian Council.

Prime Minister Bazargan and seven members of the Interim Government signed a petition to Khomeini objecting to the constitution drafted by the Assembly of Experts. They warned that it violated popular sovereignty, lacked public consensus, enshrined the clergy as a "ruling class," and would ultimately backfire by leading the public to blame every future government failure on "Islamic rule." They called the draft constitution "a revolution against the revolution," and threatened to publish their own original draft based on the French constitution.

The Interim Government had important allies for its position, including Ayatollah Shariatmadari, who had never accepted Khomeini's overreaching reinterpretation of clerical guardianship. If the public had been given a choice between the two draft constitutions, it is quite possible that Bazargan and his allies could have won that fight.

We will never know, because, at that critical moment, the United States once again intervened in Iran's affairs by admitting the Shah to the United States for cancer treatment. The public was incensed. Passions previously directed entirely at the Shah were suddenly redirected against the United States, reminding Iranians of the U.S. role in the 1953 coup and raising fears that the CIA station in the U.S. Embassy was once again plotting to impose an autocratic monarchy on Iran. Four hundred university students climbed over the wall of the U.S. Embassy and occupied it for the next 444 days, holding the American staff prisoner in their own embassy.

When Ayatollah Khomeini refused to order the students out of the embassy, Bazargan resigned, and the debate over his and Khomeini's conflicting visions for the constitution and the future of Iran was effectively over. Khomeini had won.

Important secular groups boycotted the national referendum that approved the Islamic Constitution on December 2, 1979, reducing the turnout to 75 percent from the 95 percent who had voted in the earlier referendum on the Islamic Republic. Nevertheless, the constitution was approved by 99 percent of those who voted. Few observers predicted the success, or even the survival, of the new Islamic Republic, especially when it was immediately faced with a new crisis: war with Iraq.

THE DEVASTATING IRAN-IRAQ WAR 1980–1988

The Iran-Iraq war was started by Iraqi leader Saddam Hussein, who invaded Iran in September 1980 with the aim of seizing the Arvand Rud waterway (known as Shatt al-Arab in Iraq) and Iran's oil-rich southwestern Khuzestan region.

Iran fought back fiercely. The fighters included remnants of the Shah's vaunted military, which totaled 370,000 men under arms. The new government also formed elite regiments of 120,000 Revolutionary Guards, including the super-elite 5,000-man Quds Force. In addition, it raised a volunteer force of 200,000, called Basij-e Mostazefin (Mobilization of the Oppressed), made up mostly of young boys whose homes were under attack. This militia was formed as a support force but its teenage "martyrs" were later used in "human wave" attacks against Iraqi forces.

The Iranians used the Shah's large arsenal of Western-built tanks and warplanes. Israel played a secret but critical role supporting Iran. It became a conduit for spare parts, weapons, and ammunition, keeping many of Iran's weapons operational despite a Western arms embargo.

The war ground on for a total of eight brutal years and was characterized by trench warfare comparable to the horrors of World War I, Iraqi use of chemical and biological weapons, and aerial bombardment of civilians by both sides. The death toll is estimated at somewhere between 400,000 (250,000 Iranians and 150,000 Iraqis) and a staggering one million, with Iranians suffering more of the casualties.

This tragic loss of life and several billion dollars' worth of damages finally came to an end in July 1988, with a UN-brokered ceasefire.

THE ISLAMIZATION OF IRANIAN SOCIETY

Iraq's Saddam Hussein had deliberately started the war at a time when Iran was in a state of upheaval after the 1979 Islamic Revolution. He thought the different groups vying for power would have difficulty creating a unified force to repel his army. He miscalculated, as Iran's revolutionary forces galvanized around this prolonged war with an intense sense of patriotism.

The war also provided the conditions for a massive expansion of the state's role in Iran's economy. All basic goods were rationed, alleviating some of the poverty caused by the war. Up to a quarter of the budget was dedicated to subsidies for bread, rice, sugar, cheese, fuel, cooking oil, electricity, sanitation, and water. The government opened food co-ops, took over factories abandoned by private companies, and nationalized business enterprises that had been part of the Shah's crony-capitalist patronage system. The Iranian state was soon running about 2,000 factories, many of which were losing money, but this prevented mass unemployment.

Many of the confiscated assets of the Shah, his cronies, and foreign partners were placed under the ownership of the Bonyad-e Mostazafan va Janbazan (Foundation for the Oppressed and Disabled). By the late 1980s, its assets amounted to somewhere between $10 and $20 billion, including 140 factories, 470 agribusinesses, 100 construction firms, 64 mines and 250 other companies. These included Zam Zam (the Iranian alternative to Coca-Cola and Pepsi), and the former Hilton and Hyatt hotels.

The government also expanded benefits for the working class. It passed a labor law that guaranteed many of the benefits that had been championed by the socialist Tudeh Party in the 1940s.

At the same time, it formed close ties with the bazaar merchant class, the traditional political allies of the Shiite clergy. Seventy percent of the deputies elected to the revolution's first Parliament were bazaar merchants or other members of the propertied middle class. Ayatollah Khomeini was quick to reassure these allies that the revolution would respect all forms of private property.

THE GOVERNMENT BECOMES INCREASINGLY REPRESSIVE

The war left Iranians ready for strong national leadership, and Ayatollah Khomeini stepped in to take control. The office of Supreme Leader, conceived as a religious authority to be consulted only in certain matters, came to dominate the political system. The reach of Islamic rule was extended throughout society. In the judicial system, all court rulings became subject to appeal all the way to the Guardian Council. Secular and progressive social legislation was repealed. The marriage age was lowered to 13 for girls, and men were allowed to divorce their wives without a court hearing. Women were purged from the judiciary and secular teachers fired. The Baha'i sect was persecuted, with its temples closed down and its leaders imprisoned and executed. An "Islamic code of public appearance" was enforced, favoring the chadour for women (which was later made mandatory) and requiring women to at least wear headscarves and long coats.

The "Islamization" of Iranian society was intended to affect every aspect of life. All publications were subject to censorship, textbooks were rewritten, and secular names of streets and monuments were changed.

The new government also took revenge on its opponents, especially members of the old regime. In the first two years after the revolution, the government executed about 500 of its political opponents, including a former prime minister and six cabinet ministers; 93 SAVAK officers; 205 military officers and soldiers; 35 Baha'is; and a Jewish businessman accused of spying for Israel. Many thousands were imprisoned.

Ayatollah Khomeini also attacked his former allies. Abolhassan Banisadr, for example, had been part of the anti-Shah movement since the 1960s, and returned from exile with Khomeini in 1979. Elected president in 1980, he became openly critical of the Islamic regime. He was impeached by the Parliament in 1981, apparently at the behest of Khomeini, and several of his closest friends were executed. Banisadr fled to Paris and briefly formed an alliance with the opposition group Mojahedin-e-Khalq (MEK), but fell out over the MEK's violent actions.

THE MEK'S VIOLENT RESISTANCE

The MEK, known in English as the People's Mujahideen of Iran, was formed in 1965 by a group of young people who felt the pro-democracy Freedom Movement of Iran was too moderate in its opposition to the Shah. They infused their ideology with a strange mix of Shia Islam and Marxism. When three of the original leaders were killed by the Shah's secret police, Massoud Rajavi took the leadership position.

Espousing an anti-American, anti-Imperialist agenda, while throwing their weight behind Ayatollah Khomeini, the MEK played a significant role in the revolution. From 1975 to 1979, MEK militants were reportedly involved in multiple bombings targeting military officers, government officials, and American businessmen, including the U.S. information office and the offices of Pepsi, PanAm, and General Motors.[17] The group routinely joined in calls for "Death to America" and "Death to Israel."

After the revolution, the MEK was marginalized by Khomeini. He had viewed them as useful to force the Shah from power, but later felt they were too leftist and radical to be a part of post-revolutionary Iran. He even described them as *monafeqin* (a religious term meaning hypocrites) and would not allow their leader Massoud Rajavi to run for president. The MEK boycotted the national referendum on the Islamic Republic and in 1981 declared war on the new Iranian government.

Over the course of the next few years, the hybrid Marxist-Leninist organization attacked, bombed, and assassinated members of the new Iranian leadership. In one attack in 1981, they exploded a powerful bomb during a leadership meeting of the Islamic Republic Party in Tehran. The attack killed 73 people, including Chief Justice Ayatollah Beheshti, four cabinet ministers, the speaker of the Parliament, 28 deputies, and many other important figures. Soon after that, the MEK bombed the Prime Minister's office, killing Prime Minister Mohammad Javad Bahonar, President Mohammad Ali Rajai, and six other government officials. Ali Khamenei (who later became Supreme Leader) and Akbar Hashemi Rafsanjani (who later became president) were both wounded in MEK assassination attempts. The State Department described the MEK as cutting a "swath of terror" across the country, including violent attacks on civilians.[18]

Members of the Islamic Republic's security services, essentially a ragtag group of Khomeini loyalists deputized to restore order, began cracking down on the MEK. *Hezbollahis* (as these groups were known) raided meeting places, shut down newsstands, and arrested suspected members. Much of the leadership was forced into exile in France and then in Iraq, under the protection of Iran's enemy: Saddam Hussein. In Iraq, the MEK worked with the Iraqi leader to attack Iranian positions during the Iran-Iraq war, a position viewed as treasonous by most Iranians. After the 1988 cease-fire, the MEK, backed by Iraqi warplanes, continued to attack Iran. In retaliation, the Iranian government executed MEK supporters in Iranian prisons.

The government also executed former allies from the Tudeh Party and the National Front. The moderate cleric Ayatollah Shariatmadari was stripped of his title, and he and other opposition leaders were forced to publicly recant their views. In the end, Khomeini executed or imprisoned many more former allies than he did monarchists.

Immediately after the end of the Iran-Iraq War in 1988, and a few months before his death, the Ayatollah authorized another round of mass executions. These killings have been described as a political purge without precedent in modern Iranian history. Amnesty International says that at least 2,000 political prisoners were summarily executed.[19] Iranian dissidents say the numbers were much greater, in the tens of thousands. Most were executed by hanging. Human Rights Watch said that "the deliberate and systematic manner in which these extrajudicial executions took place constitutes a crime against humanity under international law."[20]

Grand Ayatollah Montazeri, previously expected to succeed Khomeini as Supreme Leader, opposed Khomeini's wave of killing and was forced to resign. Historian Ervand Abrahamian interprets this brutal round of mass executions and Khomeini's February 1989 fatwa sentencing writer Salman Rushdie to death, a fatwa that incensed Rushdie's Western supporters, as calculated moves to forestall any accommodation with the secular opposition or the West.

Khomeini died on June 3, 1989. He was replaced by an ayatollah with a similar name, Ali Khamenei.

ATTEMPTS AT REFORM: FROM RAFSANJANI TO KHATAMI

Shortly after Khamenei became the new Supreme Leader, Ali-Akbar Hashemi Rafsanjani was elected president, running as a pragmatist against the Islamic hardliners. He was re-elected in 1993, but by a much smaller margin.

Trying to balance the budget, he launched neoliberal reforms, including abolishing rationing and price controls, opening "free trade" zones, and lowering business taxes. His free market, pro-business policies, along with falling oil prices, led to a substantial increase in foreign debt and massive inflation that intensified class differences.

His government favored renewing ties with the West as part of a strategy to secure more foreign investment and revive the country's war-torn economy. His plans to open Iran to foreign investment featured a $1 billion proposed oil deal with Conoco, a deal that was killed by an executive order from President Bill Clinton. A sanctions bill passed by the U.S. Congress further undercut Rafsanjani's opening to the West. He also alienated Western governments by relaunching Iran's nuclear energy program.

There were some cultural and social openings during his presidency, including a successful family planning program to stabilize Iran's mushrooming population. Young men and women could socialize more openly in public. Literary journals engaged in lively debates, and the film industry flourished. But these openings were attacked by conservative members of the clergy and government, and Rafsanjani's time in office was marked by repressive forces cracking down on writers, filmmakers, academics, and journalists.

The next president, Mohammad Khatami (not to be confused with the Supreme Leaders Khomeini or Khamenei), came to power in 1997 on a reformist ticket. A former minister of culture who had lived in Germany, he had been the director of the National Library and taught courses in Western political thought at Tehran University. He ran on a platform of political pluralism, free expression, and women's rights, and he reinterpreted Iranian history and national identity in more secular terms. "The essence of Iranian history is the struggle for democracy," he declared. Considered a long shot, he was elected in an upset, winning 70 percent of the votes with an 80 percent turnout.

The core of Khatami's support came from the educated middle class, college students, and the urban working class—the same classes that had provided the core support for Tudeh Party and the Mossadegh's National Front. Newspapers published by Khatami's supporters sprung up and soon outsold traditional ones, and they dramatically changed the terms of public debate. Iranian nationalism was reframed in terms that gave attention to Iran's 2,500-year history, its popular struggle against the monarchy, and the nationalization of its oil industry, not just its Islamic traditions.

Khatami and his reform agenda were wildly popular, and the reformers (including some women candidates) won 75 percent of the votes in local elections in 1999, and then 195 of the 290 parliamentary seats in 2000. Khatami was re-elected in 2001 with 80 percent of the vote. The secular leanings of the population were finally finding expression, and the clergy complained that less than two percent of Iranians attended Friday prayers at their local mosques, and less than 30 percent performed their daily prayers.

Khatami reformed some of the repressive practices of the previous era. He disbanded Intelligence Ministry death squads, reformed the prison system, reduced harassment over dress codes and entertainment, raised the marriage age to 15, and improved divorce and child custody laws. The government provided scholarships for women to study abroad, women in government jobs were allowed to wear head-scarves instead of chadours, and schoolgirls began to wear colorful clothes.

But the Guardian Council vehemently pushed back against this reform agenda. It vetoed many of the government's social reforms and disqualified 2,000 candidates, including 87 incumbents, from the next Parliamentary election. The courts shut down at least 60 progressive or secular newspapers.

Despite this pushback at home, and determined to put Iran in good stead with other world powers, Khatami made state visits to foreign capitals from Moscow to Paris to Tokyo. He hosted a conference on "dialogue among civilizations" and a human rights delegation from the European Union, and even expressed regret for the student takeover of the U.S. Embassy during the revolution. The U.K. restored diplomatic relations, President Clinton relaxed U.S. sanctions, and the UN dropped Iran from its list of countries that violate human rights. When the U.S. invaded Afghanistan in 2001, Khatami's government worked closely with the U.S. State Department to help stabilize Afghanistan after the invasion.

This forward movement was reversed, however, in January 2002 when the United States suddenly reinstated and escalated its cold war against Iran. President George W. Bush declared that Iran and North Korea were part of the same "axis of evil" as Iraq, which was already an explicit target of U.S. aggression.

Conservatives in Iran were vindicated in their opposition to improving relations with the West. Secular and progressive Iranians were disillusioned when Khatami's liberal policies were undermined by hardliners. Many progressives gave up on Khatami's brand of reformist politics as an avenue for social progress, and subsequent elections in Iran saw much lower turnout.

AHMADINEJAD AND THE SUPPRESSION OF THE GREEN MOVEMENT

President Mahmoud Ahmadinejad was elected in 2005 on a wave of conservative populism. Ahmadinejad only won six percent of the votes in the first round, but 60 percent in his final runoff with Rafsanjani, then seen by many as a corrupt, cronyist politician. Ahmadinejad ushered in a new phase of conservative policies, including a crackdown on dissent and escalating tensions with the United States.

When running for re-election for a second term in 2009, Ahmadinejad's closest contestant was the reformist and former Prime Minister Mir-Hossein Mousavi. Pundits declared they were running neck and neck. On June 13, however, the government announced Ahmadinejad the winner, insisting he received two-thirds of the votes and Mousavi only 36 percent. Mousavi's supporters cried foul.

Almost two years before the rise of the Arab Spring that rocked the Middle East, hundreds of thousands of Iranians poured into the streets of Tehran and other large cities, shouting "Where is my vote?" These protests marked the beginning of what came to be called the Green Movement. (Green was the color used by Mousavi's campaign, but after the election it became the symbol of the pro-democracy movement.)

Two days after the election, the Supreme Leader Khamenei disappointed the protesters by endorsing the results. Undaunted, the next day Mousavi supporters staged a massive protest of some three million people, the largest protest ever since the 1979 revolution. This protest and subsequent ones were met with riot police and the Basij paramilitary militia armed with bats and chains. The government not only beat and arrested protesters, but raided the homes of prominent reformist politicians and journalists, dragging them off to prison. Mousavi was placed under house arrest.

Citizen journalists began filming the protests and the crackdowns, broadcasting the uprising to the world community. On June 20, the video of a young university student named Neda Agha-Soltan, shot in the chest by a rooftop sniper, went viral. Neda Agha-Soltan became known as one of the many martyrs who died in the pro-democracy movement.

What began as a call for a recount of the votes turned into a call for an end to the Islamic Republic. The protests continued for 20 months, and so did the repression. The government portrayed the Green Movement as a creation of the United States with the goal of destroying the Islamic state, and held show trials where leaders were forced to confess to crimes against the nation. Thousands of dissidents fled, moving mostly to Europe and North America. Newspapers, magazines, and websites were shut down. Iran became the country with the most journalists in prison.

By February 2011, faced with radicalized protesters and massive state repression, including torture in prisons and even executions, the movement's leaders halted calls for more demonstrations. The movement receded from public space into the underground. Its leaders, including Mousavi and former Speaker of Parliament Mehdi Karroubi, were still under house arrest in 2017, due to the intransigence of the Supreme Leader and some of the Revolutionary Guard commanders.

The Green Movement was defeated, but it sowed the seeds that led to the rise of reformist President Hassan Rouhani in 2013, a moderate who encouraged more personal freedom and improved diplomatic relations with the West. Rouhani was re-elected in 2017, but his government also faced pushback from conservatives and a December 2017 uprising among youth and working class people frustrated by economic hardships.

CHANGE THROUGH THE ELECTORAL PROCESS

Despite the profoundly undemocratic pre-election vetting of presidential candidates by Iran's Guardian Council and the power invested in unelected leaders, elections in Iran are serious contests and do matter. Elections are highly contested and unpredictable. Although reformist candidates are often not allowed to run, candidates with varied platforms have made it through the vetting. Iranian elections usually have large turnouts (over 70 percent) because it is one of the few opportunities people have to weigh in on the direction of their country.

Some opposition political parties do exist, such as the reformist Mardom Salari party and the Etemad Melli party, but their members face harassment and their leaders are often arrested.

Most candidates do not belong to political parties but to political factions or alliances. These groups lack the formal structure of political parties but compete just as fiercely. When running for office, some candidates are backed by more than one group, and allegiances often shift. There are factions representing hardline religious interests, pro-reform factions (whose candidates are often disqualified), and pragmatists that fall in the middle of Iran's political spectrum.

The people's desire for reform can be seen in their voting patterns. An analysis of Iran's presidential elections led author/analyst Trita Parsi to conclude that, despite the near limitless powers ascribed to the Supreme Leader, the anti-establishment vote has tended to dominate Iranian elections.[21] In 1997, the Speaker of the Parliament, Ali Akbar Nategh Nouri, was seen as favored by Ayatollah Khamenei, but the Iranian people instead gave their support to a largely unknown reformist candidate, Mohammad Khatami. Eight years later, another unknown candidate, Mahmoud Ahmadinejad, won the anti-establishment vote over the late Ali Akbar Hashemi Rafsanjani, who was perceived as the establishment candidate.

By 2009, the roles had reversed. Ahmadinejad was the establishment candidate running for re-election while Mir Hossein Mousavi, who resurfaced after more than two decades of internal political exile, was considered the anti-establishment candidate. That's why there was such a public outcry when Mousavi was not declared the winner. Again in 2013, the candidate perceived to have the Supreme Leader's support, Saeed Jalili, lost to reform candidate Hassan Rouhani.

Unlike the Supreme Leader, presidents must actually appeal to the electorate directly and are held accountable for policies that affect people's daily lives. The unelected power structures, including the Supreme Leader, the military, judiciary, and intelligence agencies, are often suspicious of the president and try to keep him from gaining too much power.

This power play between Iran's elected and unelected forces will determine Iran's future. The nation's transformation to a truly democratic system will only come with the elimination of the position of Supreme Leader and the clerical bodies under his control. On the other hand, people should not underestimate the political openings that do exist, making Iran one of the more democratic societies in the Middle East.

HOW POWER IS DIVIDED AMONG OFFICIAL GOVERNMENT ENTITIES

An organizational chart of Iran's institutions shows two completely different systems, one democratic and the other theocratic.

While the system is supposed to be a combination of democratic involvement with theocratic oversight, the two often clash, with unelected, unaccountable officials holding the most power.

THE SUPREME LEADER

At the top of Iran's power structure is the Supreme Leader, who is appointed by the Assembly of Experts for this lifetime position. The father of the Iranian Revolution Ayatollah Ruhollah Khomeini and his successor Ayatollah Ali Khamenei, who became Leader upon Khomeini's death in 1989, are the only two men to have held this office since the founding of the Islamic Republic in 1979.

According to Iran's constitution, the Supreme Leader is responsible for setting the direction of Iran's domestic and foreign policies. The Supreme Leader is also commander-in-chief of the armed forces and controls the Islamic Republic's intelligence and security operation. He is the only one who can declare war or peace. Iran is the only state in the world in which the executive branch does not control the armed forces.

The Supreme Leader has the power to appoint and dismiss the leaders of the judiciary, the state radio and television networks, and the Islamic Revolutionary Guard Corps. He also appoints six of the twelve members of the Guardian Council, the powerful body that oversees the activities of Parliament and determines which candidates are qualified to run for public office. The foundations, called *bonyads*, that operate hundreds of companies, are also under the Supreme Leader's control.

The Supreme Leader's sphere of power is extended through his representatives, an estimated 2,000 of whom are sprinkled throughout all sectors of the government and who serve as the Leader's field operatives. His representatives are often more powerful than the president's ministers, since they have the authority to intervene in any matter of state on the Supreme Leader's behalf.

THE PRESIDENT

The president is the second highest ranking official, after the Supreme Leader, and the highest ranking elected official. The president is elected by popular vote for four years and can serve two consecutive terms. Eight vice presidents serve under the president, as well as a cabinet of 22 ministers that must be confirmed by Parliament.

The executive branch is subordinate to the Supreme Leader. Though the president has nominal rule over the Supreme National Security Council and the Ministry of Intelligence and Security, in practice the Supreme Leader is in charge of most foreign and domestic security matters.

Despite these restrictions, over the years the presidency has evolved into a powerful office. One reason is that there used to be a prime minister as well, a position more powerful than the president, but that post was abolished in the 1989 constitutional amendment. Every president that followed has put his stamp on domestic and foreign policies.

THE PARLIAMENT

The Iranian Parliament, called the *Majlis*, is a unicameral legislative body made up of 290 members who are publicly elected every four years. The Parliament drafts legislation, ratifies international treaties, and approves the country's budget. It is also empowered to investigate complaints against the executive branch and the judiciary, approve the president's choice of cabinet ministers, and appoint six members of the 12-person Guardian Council. By a two-thirds majority, it can initiate referenda on proposed amendments to the constitution.

Parliamentary sessions are open to the public; its deliberations are broadcast and its minutes are published.

While reformist candidates tend to win most of the seats and in recent years only a small percentage of the elected deputies have been clerics, the Parliament is still held in check by the Guardian Council, the influential oversight body that examines all laws passed by Parliament to determine their compatibility with sharia law. Over the years, the council has struck down hundreds of laws passed by Parliament.

ASSEMBLY OF EXPERTS

The Assembly of Experts is an obscure governing body that only meets for one week every year. It consists of 86 "virtuous and learned" clerics elected by the public to eight-year terms. Like presidential and parliamentary elections, the Guardian Council determines who can run for a seat in this Assembly of Experts.

Members of the Assembly of Experts in turn elect the Supreme Leader from within their own ranks and periodically reconfirm him. The assembly has never been known to challenge any of the Supreme Leader's decisions or to deny reconfirmation.

GUARDIAN COUNCIL

Twelve jurists comprise the Guardian Council. The Supreme Leader appoints half; the head of the judiciary recommends the remaining six, which are officially appointed by Parliament. All serve for six-year terms.

The Guardian Council has the authority to interpret the constitution and determine if the laws passed by Parliament are in line with Islamic law. This gives the council effective veto power over Parliament. The Council consistently vetoes laws passed by the popularly elected Parliament. If it deems that a law passed by Parliament is incompatible with the constitution or Islamic law, the law is referred back to Parliament for revision. If the Parliament and the Guardian Council cannot decide on a case, it is passed to the Expediency Council for a decision.

The council also has tremendous power over the president and Parliament because it is the body that vets candidates to determine who is "competent" to run and who is not. The Council favors conservative candidates and typically disqualifies most reform candidates. No one who is perceived to be an opponent or critic of the Islamic system is permitted to run for president, and no woman has ever been approved as a presidential candidate. After conservative candidates fared poorly in the 2000 parliamentary elections, the Council disqualified more than 3,600 reformist and independent candidates for the 2004 elections.

In the 2009 election, 476 men and women applied to the Guardian Council to seek the presidency, and only four were approved. Among the arbitrary reasons for disqualifying candidates, without having to furnish any proof, are narcotics addiction or involvement in drug-smuggling, connections to the Shah's pre-revolutionary government, lack of belief in or insufficient practice of Islam, being against the Islamic Republic, or having connections to foreign intelligence services.

EXPEDIENCY COUNCIL

In 1988, when stalemates between Parliament and the Guardian Council proved intractable, Ayatollah Khomeini created the

Expediency Council and charged it with mediating disputes between the two bodies. Now, according to the constitution, the Expediency Council serves as an advisory body to the Supreme Leader.

The council is made up of 34 members who tend to come mostly from the conservative factions. It usually sides with the conservative Guardian Council in its disputes with Parliament, which is why some parliamentary leaders have called for the council to be reformed.

JUDICIARY

The judicial branch of Iran's government is largely controlled by the Supreme Leader, who appoints the head of the judiciary, who in turn appoints the head of the Supreme Court and the chief public prosecutor.

Public courts deal with civil and criminal cases. There are Special Clerical Courts, which function independently of the regular judicial framework, and handle crimes allegedly committed by clerics. There are also "revolutionary courts" that try certain categories of offenses, including crimes against national security, narcotics smuggling, and acts deemed to undermine the Islamic Republic. Decisions rendered in revolutionary courts are final and cannot be appealed.

IRANIAN ARMED FORCES

The Armed Forces consists of the Army, Navy, and the Air Force. There are reportedly about 520,000 Iranians on active service, including 350,000 in the army.

According to Iran's constitution, the regular army is responsible for guarding the independence and territorial integrity of the country and maintaining order. The army falls under the control of the Supreme Leader.

The Islamic Revolutionary Guard Corps, or IRGC, was created in 1979 by Ayatollah Khomeini to protect the revolution and its achievements. It is separate from the regular military, and there has been a rivalry between the two military branches since the founding of the Islamic Republic.

There are about 120,000 members of the IRGC, and it has its own Navy, Air Force, Ground Forces, and Quds Force (special forces). The IRGC also controls the paramilitary volunteer force called *Basij*, which is thought to have about 90,000 active-duty members and 300,000 reservists. The Basij claims is also has a membership of 12 million men and women who are ready to mobilize if/when the need arises, but some outside experts put that figure at 500,000.

The IRGC was put in charge of the military industry. It poured money into the development of its own tanks, radar systems, guided missiles, military vessels, fighter planes, and drones.

Over the years, the IRGC has become among the most autonomous power centers in Iran. In 1982, it sent troops to Lebanon in support of the militant group Hezbollah, and it has since become active in supporting Islamic revolutionary movements in other parts of the Muslim world. It supports Palestinian militant groups in the West Bank, including the Palestinian Islamic Jihad, and Hamas.

MINISTRY OF INTELLIGENCE & SECURITY (MOIS)

The Ministry of Intelligence and Security (MOIS) is a shadowy entity under the control of the Supreme Leader. A special law dictates that the head of the MOIS must be a cleric, which deepens the Supreme Leader's influence.

The ministry is tasked with the "gathering, procurement, analysis, and classification of necessary information inside and outside the country" and disclosing conspiracies that could sabotage the integrity of the Islamic Republic.

The MOIS is infamous for eliminating political dissidents within Iran's borders and plays a key role in organizing and conducting terrorist operations abroad, running operations out of Iranian embassies, consulates, and Islamic centers overseas.

CHAPTER 3: THE STRUGGLE FOR HUMAN RIGHTS IN IRAN

If asked "What first comes to mind when you think about Iran?", many people, especially in the U.S., would list human rights violations. Very few would know that the empire of ancient Persia, now the state of Iran, actually set the precedent of human rights in 539 B.C. when Cyrus the Great conquered Babylon. In a major step forward for humankind, this conqueror set the slaves free and granted them the right to return home, declared that all people had the right to choose their own religion, and established a system of racial equality. Not only did Cyrus the Great take the first stand for establishing these human rights, he actually documented them on a barrel-shaped baked clay tablet inscribed in Babylonian cuneiform writing (now known as the Cyrus Cylinder). This ancient record has been officially recognized as the first human rights charter. The United Nations has translated the text into all six official languages and used it as the basis of the first four articles of the Universal Declaration of Human Rights.[22]

Iran today, unfortunately, is no bastion of freedom. The Islamic Republic has a disastrous track record, ranging from violations of religious freedom and women's rights to the use of torture and capital punishment. On a scale of 100, Freedom House ranks Iran near the bottom, with an abysmal score of 17.[23]

The early years of the revolution were the worst, when moral puritanism swept through the nation. Thousands of prostitutes, drug addicts, and homosexuals were executed. In public places, revolutionaries confronted people who failed to abide by the strict new codes of dress and behavior. Prison sentences and flogging became commonplace for the most minor moral indiscretions, and government offices were purged of the ideologically "unsound." The abuses were amplified when Iraq's army crossed the border into Iran in 1980, leading to a bloody decade of war with Iraq and brutal crackdowns at home.

While the situation has since improved, especially during reform governments, the Iranian government continues to severely restrict civil liberties, including freedoms of assembly, association, speech, religion, and press. There is a lack of due process within the country's legal system, and the government condones the use of torture and capital punishment. The government persecutes human rights defenders, journalists, and trade union leaders. Also facing persecution are religious and ethnic minorities, as well as people of alternative sexualities.

This chapter gives an overview of the human rights situation, highlighting the many violations but also the valiant work of dedicated Iranian activists, at home and abroad, who strive to open more spaces for Iranians to exercise their basic rights.

WHAT RIGHTS DID IRANIANS HAVE UNDER THE SHAH?

Lest one thinks that Iran went from a Western-style form of governance under the Shah to a theocratic dictatorship, it's important to recall the brutality of the Shah's rule. The Shah systematically dismantled the judicial system and violated people's personal liberties. Military courts tried as "terrorists" those brave enough to protest his regime. His infamous intelligence agency SAVAK carried out torture under that friendly guidance of the CIA, which set up SAVAK in 1957 and taught Iranians how to interrogate suspects. The Shah kept tens of thousands of dissidents holed up in prison, where the methods of torture included "whipping and beating, electric shocks, extraction of teeth and nails, boiling water pumped into the rectum, heavy weights hung on the testicles, tying the prisoner to a metal table heated to a white heat, inserting a broken bottle into the anus, and rape."[24]

WHAT HUMAN RIGHTS DOES THE IRANIAN GOVERNMENT RECOGNIZE?

When the revolution came to power, it rewrote the old 1905 constitution. The new constitution, which was amended in 1989, contains a hybrid of theocratic and democratic elements. It recognizes many key human rights, including equal rights for racial and ethnic minorities, gender equality, freedom of association, freedom of expression, and freedom of the press.

At first glance, these guarantees look promising, but there are stipulations and reservations that run counter to these promises. The constitution includes phrases such as "unless the law states otherwise" and "unless they attack the principles of Islam," which leaves the population vulnerable to the whims of interpretation.[25]

Iran was one of the original 51 member states that founded the United Nations in 1951. Since then, it has ratified many of the international declarations relating to human rights, including the Covenant on Economic, Social and Cultural Rights, the International Convention on the Elimination of All Forms of Racial Discrimination, and the International Covenant on Civil and Political Rights. The Convention on the Rights of the Child, a document the United States has never signed, was ratified in 1994. The government also signed additional protocols against child trafficking, child prostitution, child pornography, and the involvement of children in armed conflict. Once again, however, these conventions and covenants were ratified with the catch-all reservation that Iran will adhere to them as long as they are in accordance with Islamic principles.

Iran has not signed the Convention on the Elimination of All Forms of Discrimination Against Women (CEDAW), making it one of only seven countries out of the UN's 194 member states failing to do so (one of the other non-signatories is the United States). The Iranian Parliament discussed signing CEDAW, but the Council of Guardians ruled that the legislation would be "un-Islamic." Iran also refused to sign the Convention Against Torture or adopt the UN protocol abolishing the death penalty.

In December 2016, the government adopted a Charter on Citizens' Rights. It recognizes the right of every citizen to freedom of speech and expression, and the right to freely seek, receive, and publish information using any means of communication. The charter, however, is not legally binding, and the government continues to disrespect these rights.

WHAT ABOUT FREEDOM OF SPEECH, ASSOCIATION, AND ASSEMBLY?

The Iranian constitution claims freedom of expression, but in reality all forms of media, from local magazines to international broadcasts via satellite, are subject to the authorities' discretion. The government has shut down numerous publications, and journalists are regularly subjected to interrogation, surveillance, arrest, and other forms of harassment and intimidation. The government also bans many social media outlets and smartphone applications. Among those regularly blocked are Facebook, Twitter, WhatsApp, Line, Instagram Live, and Tango, although Iranians are very clever at finding ways to counter government interference.[26]

Unfortunately, Iranians have also been blocked from social media by the U.S. side. In 2017, Apple removed a number of popular Iranian apps from its app stores to comply with U.S. sanctions.

Cultural workers also face repression for peacefully exercising their right to free expression. While the Iranian film industry thrives and is acclaimed internationally, films may be censored or banned, and filmmakers arrested. Filmmaker Keyvan Karimi spent five months in prison in 2016 after he was convicted of "propagating against the ruling system" and "insulting religious sanctities" because of a documentary he made about political graffiti.

Music was totally banned at the start of the revolution. Then classical music was allowed on radio and TV stations, with some public concerts held in the late 1980s. In the 1990s, under reformist President Khatami, restrictions were further relaxed. Today, there is a flourishing music scene, but censorship persists. Concerts get canceled, and musicians can be arrested for the content of their music. After a 15-minute trial, music producers Mehdi and Hossein Rajabian were sentenced to six years in prison (reduced to three years on appeal) in 2015 for "insulting the sacred" and "propaganda against the state."[27]

In terms of free association, the constitution says that the formation of political parties, societies, and political or professional associations is permitted, but then adds the usual caveat "provided they do not violate the principles of independence, freedom, national unity, the criteria of Islam or the basis of the Islamic Republic."[28] According to the Interior Ministry, there are over 250 registered political parties or associations. Most are not parties in the Western sense, with membership and detailed party platforms, but more like interest groups and factions. Many appear at election time and then disappear. Parties that oppose the Islamic Revolution are either banned or severely restricted.

NGOs must be registered (as is most countries) and are monitored by the state. The government allows charity and social service organizations, such as those dedicated to helping the poor or sheltering abused women, but routinely cracks down on groups involved in political activities. Severe restrictions on freedom of expression prevent civic groups from openly criticizing state policies. The government is also particularly suspicious of groups with international partners, especially if the international partner is from the United States.

Government-sponsored rallies abound, but permits for non-governmental groups to hold rallies or demonstrations are routinely denied. Protesters, especially students and ethnic minorities demanding human rights, risk government surveillance, harassment, arrest, and imprisonment.

There is a fine line between what is permitted and what is prohibited, and the fate of civic groups is often determined by the government in power and the larger political situation. The reform years of President Khatami from 1997–2005, for example, gave rise to independent civil society organizations of workers, intellectuals, students, and women. After Ahmadinejad was elected in 2005, these public spaces came under attack. Some of the most prominent NGOs were shut down, including the Center for the Defense of Human Rights, led by Nobel Peace Prize winner Shirin Ebadi, and the Organization for the Defense of Prisoners' Rights, led by Emad Baghi. Ebadi ended up leaving Iran, and Baghi was imprisoned on charges of working against national security.

After the Green Movement in 2009, the government crackdown was more severe. Peaceful protests by hundreds of thousands in Tehran were put down brutally. Thousands were detained and more than 100 accused in a televised mass show trial. Prominent opposition leaders were placed under house arrest. These were reformist politician and cleric Mehdi Karroubi;

Mir Hossein Mousavi, former prime minister whose electoral challenge to President Ahmadinejad's re-election sparked the Green Movement; and Mousavi's wife—and women's rights advocate—Zahra Rahnavard. They were punished for publicly disputing the election results and leading peaceful mass demonstrations.

The protests that started in December 2017 and spread throughout the country were also crushed by the policy and Revolutionary Guards, with over 1,000 arrests.

Despite the dangers, there are all sorts of civic groups, many of which come and go depending on the level of government pressure they attract. The Internet has provided new means of collaboration and information sharing, creating conditions for a more diverse range of organizations, but government surveillance of the Internet makes online organizing risky as well.

IMPRISONMENT OF FOREIGNERS AND IRANIANS WITH DUAL NATIONALITY

Particularly volatile have been the arrests of foreigners and dual nationals—people who are citizens of both Iran and another country. Most live overseas and have been arrested, while visiting Iran, on charges related to espionage. Some might well be spies, some are used for prisoner swaps, and others are victims of paranoia against Westerners by Iranian hardliners. The Iranian government does not recognize dual nationality, so when these people are detained they are usually denied access to the services of the embassy where they reside.

A particularly brutal case occurred in 2003, when Iranian-Canadian photojournalist Zahra Kazemi was arrested while taking pictures of grieving mothers outside of Iran's Evin Prison. During her detention, Iranian prison authorities severely tortured her, breaking several bones and allegedly sexually abusing her.

Kazemi was eventually taken to a hospital with internal bleeding and a brain injury. While she was in a coma at the hospital, Iranian officials initially failed to contact Canadian consular officials and refused to allow her family access to her. Kazemi died in the hospital; even then, the Iranian government ignored the wishes of Canadian officials and her family that her remains be returned to Canada for burial.[29]

In 2009, Iranian-American freelance journalist Roxana Saberi was arrested for spying, and held for over 100 days. (Her original sentence was eight years.) Another journalist, Iranian-Canadian Maziar Bahari, was arrested while covering the 2009 Iranian election for *Newsweek* and held for 118 days. That was the same year three American hikers—Joshua Fattal, Sarah Shourd, and Shane Bauer—were arrested on trumped-up charges of espionage after accidentally crossing the Iraq border into Iran, and remained imprisoned until 2011. Their two-year ordeal aggravated relations with the United States, and was seen as part of a tragic power play between the Iranian president, who wanted the Americans released, and the conservative judiciary who wanted to embarrass him.

Several similar cases occurred in 2016, just after the Iran nuclear deal was signed. It was seen as part of a power struggle playing out within the government, pitting reformist President Rouhani against hardliners who wanted to sabotage his openings to the West. An Iranian-American father and son, Baquer and Siamak Namazi, were both sentenced to ten years in prison for "collusion with the enemy state." A young British-Iranian woman, Nazanin Zaghari-Ratcliffe, was arrested in 2016 on her way back to England with her two-year-old daughter. She was sentenced to five years for spreading propaganda following a trial in which her lawyer had only five minutes to argue her defense and she was not allowed to speak.[30] Homa Hoodfar, an Iranian-Canadian academic, was also detained in 2016, then released after a few months.

Perhaps the best known recent case was that of Jason Rezian, an Iranian-American correspondent for the *Washington Post*, who was arrested in 2014 on charges that included spying. He was released in 2016 as part of a prison exchange between the U.S. and Iran.

HOW FAIR IS THE JUDICIAL SYSTEM?

Prior to the Iranian Revolution of 1979, Iran's judicial system was overseen by the Pahlavi Dynasty, and over the course of the 20th century leading up to 1979, the system was largely westernized and secularized, with a constitution that recognized both secular and sharia judiciary authority. Different areas of the law were divided into distinct courts that operated independently, with some cases relegated to the military courts and others to the clerics.

The 1979 revolution led to an overhaul of the legal system to fully incorporate Islamic law. Sharia law is the legal system for Islam that derives from the Quran, Islam's holy text, and the *Sunnah*, or religious traditions based on the sayings of the Prophet Muhammad. It acts as a code of conduct governing many aspects of the personal and public lives of Muslims. The judges are clerics trained in Islamic jurisprudence, and women are banned from being judges.

In addition to problems caused by merging the legal system with religious beliefs, many laws were written in vague terms that then allowed for subjective interpretations and contradictory rulings. Arrests are often made on arbitrary or ambiguous charges, which leads to biased and unfair trials. Trials can move forward without evidence and without conforming to fundamental standards of due process.

Amnesty International has reported that defense lawyers are regularly barred from obtaining case files and meeting directly with their clients before the trial.[31] Within the courts, the testimony of a man is often given twice the weight of that of a woman, and for certain offenses, the testimony of a woman is not even accepted. Detainees are often held in solitary confinement for long periods of time and denied contact with family or a lawyer. Iranian courts accept confessions extracted through torture.

In June 2015, Iran adopted a new, much awaited, criminal procedure code that addressed many flaws in the old code. While the new code stipulates the right to counsel from the moment of arrest through to trial and relative improvements for defense attorneys and the accused, a last minute move by Parliament provided that only selective lawyers may intervene during certain investigations. This provision effectively separated lawyers into two groups—those who are approved by the judiciary and security services, and those who are not.

WHAT ARE THE PRISON CONDITIONS LIKE AND HOW COMMON IS THE USE OF TORTURE?

Iran's prison systems are infamous for their use of torture, especially against detainees during interrogation in order to intimidate them into giving a confession. Common methods of torture include floggings and brutal beatings; more rare are blinding, burnings, and amputations. Other forms of abuse within Iranian prisons—sometimes called "white torture"—is psychological torture that ranges from solitary confinement, sleep deprivation, threats of execution or rape, sexual harassment, virginity tests, and electroshock. Denial of access to proper and necessary medical treatment for detainees is also widely reported. In some cases, depriving a prisoner of medical care is used as a form of punishment.

After the 2009 Green Movement uprising, four detainees died after being tortured in Tehran's Kahrizak Detention Center. Other detainees emerged with stories of rape, torture, and appalling conditions. Ebrahim Sharifi, a 24-year-old student from Tehran, told Amnesty that he was bound, blindfolded and beaten prior to being raped. He also endured severe beatings, and mock executions.[32]

Overcrowding in prisons is also a problem, as it is in prisons around the world. Prisoners may be forced to sleep on floors, in hallways, or in prison yards. In 2016, a member of the National Assembly reported that there were 400,000 prisoners in prisons built for 140,000.

Solitary confinement is a common method used in Iran's prisons to force confessions or to break prisoners. "I haven't experienced death but I think this is how it must feel; in an instant, you are cut off from everything and everyone," said Abbas Hakemzadeh, a student activist who fled Iran after three arrests, including 190 days in solitary.[33]

The three American hikers arrested in 2009 were held in solitary confinement for the first four months of their harrowing ordeal. Upon their release, they made it a point to campaign against solitary confinement in U.S. prisons, once they discovered that U.S. prisons held 80,000 prisoners in solitary in 2005, the last year the federal government released such data. They thought it was important to show that the United States, a country that prides itself on its democratic values, also makes widespread use of a form of punishment that many consider torture.

HOW OFTEN IS THE DEATH PENALTY CARRIED OUT?

The Iranian government has deemed capital punishment a reasonable form of justice not only for violent crimes, but also for nonviolent crimes. After China, Iran executes more people than any other country in the world; when judged on a per capita basis, Iran has the dubious distinction of being number one worldwide. The most common method of execution is hanging, although shooting and stoning have also been used.

Stoning was used in the past as a horrific penalty for adultery. According to this barbaric practice, the convicted offender—woman or man, sometimes both—is partially buried and then bludgeoned to death. Iranian women's groups, along with outside human rights organizations, fought long and hard to end this. World criticism reached a fevered pitch in 2011 when a married woman, Sakieneh Mohammadi Ashtiani, was about to be stoned over "illicit relationships" with two men. The stoning was halted.

A campaign called "Stop Stoning Forever," an initiative of the group Women Living Under Muslim Laws, was successful in getting the Iranian government to prohibit the practice, but lower courts in rural areas still sometimes hand down this dreadful sentence. The last reported case of stoning was in 2009, when a man was stoned to death in the northern city of Rasht.

There are no precise statistics on executions in Iran because the government doesn't publish the figures, but various human rights groups try to cull the information. In the first six months of 2017, the UN said 247 people had been killed, including three women. The number of executions carried out in 2016 is estimated at between 500–600, meaning that at least one person was killed by the state every day. In 2015, the number was even higher—some say over 900, the highest in more than two decades. The vast majority of executions, about 70 percent, are for drug-related offenses, and those executed are mainly poor people from marginalized groups.

Some of the crimes that warrant the death penalty are similar to those in other countries that sanction state killing: premeditated murder, rape, armed robbery, kidnapping, and drug trafficking. Other crimes are more political and religious. Anybody who commits treason, espionage, or a major crime against domestic security or external security may be charged with "corruption on earth, " which can carry the death penalty. Moral crimes that can carry the death penalty include adultery, apostasy, blasphemy against the Prophet, incest, homosexual relations, and publishing pornography.

The UN Special Rapporteur for Human Rights has called on Iran to place a general moratorium on the use of the death penalty, replace the death penalty for drug-related offences with penalties that comply with international standards, and end the practice of public executions.[34]

DOES IRAN EXECUTE JUVENILES?

Although Iran signed the UN Convention on the Rights of the Child, it continues to violate the basic rights of minors. In fact, Iran is the world's top executioner of convicted minors.[35] The penal code was supposedly changed in 2012 to end child execution, but the law still defines puberty, which is age 15 for boys and nine for girls, as the benchmark for when a death sentence can be legally imposed. Minors languish in prison from the time of their conviction until they are 18 when the sentence can be carried out. This was the case for 15-year-old Shaqayeq, who was sentenced to death for the armed robbery of a convenience store.[36] At the end of 2015, at least 160 juveniles were on death row. Human rights groups around the world have called on Iran to immediately end the sentencing of children to death and to commute the death sentences of all children on death row.

HOW ARE ETHNIC MINORITIES TREATED?

Discrimination against ethnic minorities has a long history in Iran. During the time of the Shah, millions of Kurds, Turks, Arabs, Baluchis, and Turkmen were deprived of the right to learn in their mother tongues, and no cultural expression or publication was allowed in their languages. Precisely because of this discriminiation, many ethnic minority activists joined the revolution, but felt bitterly betrayed when the new Islamic government continued the same repressive policies.

Ethnic minority groups are routinely denied the ability to express their cultural heritage, seek adequate housing and employment, or run for political office. In 2016, the government announced that optional Turkish and Kurdish language courses would be offered in schools in two provinces, Kurdistan and West Azerbaijan. That same year, however, three Arab ethnic rights activists were sentenced to a year in prison for organizing Arabic-language classes, and four Azeris were imprisoned on charges of "assembly and collusion against national security" for peacefully advocating the teaching of their mother tongues in local schools.

The limited access to education and employment continues a cycle of economic instability and marginalization for many minorities. If individuals from these minority groups speak out against the violations of their rights, the government often responds with arbitrary arrests, unfair trials, imprisonment, torture, and—in some instances—the death penalty.

One repressed minority are the Baluchis. This group is largely Sunni Muslims, which has contributed to tension with Iran's Shiite government. Baluchis are noticeably underrepresented in government positions. In 2003, a group of Baluchis formed Jundallah, a militant group that organized attacks against government soldiers and seized hostages to dramatize their plight. The government cracked down on Jundallah, as well as on Baluchi journalists and human rights activists.

The Kurds have had the most active separatist movements. Soon after the revolution, they launched a militant movement that was crushed in 1981 by the Iranian army and the Revolutionary Guards. Iranian Kurds have been executed or given long prison sentences for being members or sympathizers of militant groups. The conflict has spilled overseas, where Iranian intelligence agents allegedly killed Kurdish opposition leaders in Vienna in 1989 and Berlin in 1992.

Most Kurdish activists now use nonviolent tactics. When Kurds in Iraq held a non-binding referendum on independence in 2017, Iranian Kurds celebrated in solidarity. Some were arrested for "participation in illegal gatherings and disturbing public order."

Almost all of these minority groups live on the borders, and they often become pawns in larger geopolitical struggles. The United States and Israel have supported separatist groups to destabilize Iran. For the most part, however, Iran's ethnic minorities are less interested in secession or independence—they are more interested in increasing their rights as Iranian citizens.

HOW DOES THE GOVERNMENT TREAT HUMAN RIGHTS ACTIVISTS?

Iranians have a strong history of activism, both pre- and post-revolution. Despite the risks, there are active student groups, journalists advocating the right to free speech, lawyers defending dissidents and promoting the rights of prisoners, women's rights advocates, anti-death penalty activists, and more. Human rights advocates also denounce corruption and impunity within the police forces, and try to stop the police from using violence against protesters.

In Iran today, however, human rights activists are subjected to arrests, interrogations, threats, torture, unfair trials, and other forms of harsh punishment. Of all the prisoners detained in Iran, about 800 are considered by human rights groups to be political prisoners, incarcerated for their activism in pursuit of fundamental human rights.[37]

Iran's government is quick to label opposition groups, political activists, and promoters of human rights as terrorists. In Amnesty International's 2016 country report, the group noted that the authorities had intensified their repression of human rights defenders, subjecting protesters to beatings and arbitrary detention, sentencing them to long prison terms for charges such as "gathering and colluding against national security." The government has also taken action against the families and lawyers of activists and dissidents in order to exert pressure on them.

Organizations are often shut down if the authorities disapprove of their activities. The Association of Iranian Journalists, created in 1997 under the Khatami reform period to protect journalists' rights, was shut down in 2009, but journalists continue to push for its reinstatement. In 2015 they wrote an open letter to President Rouhani calling on him to fulfill his 2013 campaign promise to lift the ban on their organization, but the group remains banned.

Student groups are also active campaigners for student rights. In 2013, 92 student groups rallied together to call for an end of the government's repressive hold on universities.[38]

Among the prominent human rights activists in prison as of 2018 is lawyer Abdolfattah Soltani, who received an 18-year prison sentence in 2012 for his work at the Center for Human Rights Defenders, and for spreading anti-government propaganda, endangering national security, and accepting an illegal prize, the Nuremberg International Human Rights Award. Amnesty International designated him a prisoner of conscience and called him "one of the bravest human rights defenders in Iran."[39] Among well-known women prisoners is Narges Mohammadi, who in 2015 was sentenced to 16 years in prison. The judge found her guilty of "gathering and conspiring with the aim of committing crimes against national security," sentencing her to five years in prison. He added one year for "propaganda against the state" and 10 years for "forming and managing an illegal group." The group, called Legham, was an organization advocating to abolish the death penalty.[40]

Many outside groups support these courageous human rights defenders in Iran, including Amnesty International, Human Rights Watch, United for Iran, the International Campaign for Human Rights in Iran, and the Center for Human Rights in Iran. They help inform the international community, keep track of prisoners, and pressure the government for their release. Without these organizations, it would be even more difficult to know about the plight of human rights activists and how to advocate on their behalf.

CHAPTER 4: "SOCIAL DEVIANTS": GAYS, PROSTITUTES, DRUGS, AND ALCOHOL

In Iran's strict, religious society, people who live outside the "moral norm" set down by the religious authorities live difficult lives. This includes people in the LGBTQ community and people who engage in illicit activities such as prostitution or drug use/dealing. The Iranian government considers these people deviants who have lost the balanced and natural human condition.

HOW DOES THE GOVERNMENT TREAT THE LGBTQ COMMUNITY?

Iran is infamous for repression against people who are not heterosexual. When President Mahmoud Ahmadinejad gave a talk at Columbia University in New York in 2007, he earned widespread condemnation when he replied to a question about gays by saying, "In Iran we don't have homosexuals like in your country. This does not exist in our country." A government spokesperson later insisted that the translation was incorrect. The president didn't mean that there were *no* homosexuals but that there weren't as *many* as in the United States. In any case, the comment was more a reflection of the regime's wishes than the reality. There are certainly many people of various sexual tendencies in Iran, just like in any society.

Before the 1979 revolution, homosexuality was technically illegal but largely tolerated, particularly in large cities. After the revolution, discrimination against non-heterosexual people was based on the notion that such behavior is forbidden by the state's religion. Some of Iran's clerics describe homosexuality as "moral bankruptcy" or "modern Western barbarism."

Being convicted of homosexuality/homosexual acts is punishable by imprisonment, flogging, or even execution. Iran is one of six countries globally where same-sex relationships can carry the death penalty. The other five are Saudi Arabia, Sudan, Yemen, Nigeria, and Somalia.[41]

Hundreds of people have been executed on the basis of their sexual identity, mostly in the early years of the revolution. It still occurs, but usually along with other charges such as male rape and usually in more remote parts of the country. In 2016, a 19-year-old boy, Hassan Afshar, was convicted of raping another teenager and was executed by hanging in Arak Prison in Iran's Markazi Province. He was a 17-year-old high school student when he was arrested. According to Amnesty International, "He had no access to a lawyer and the judiciary rushed through the investigation and prosecution, convicting and sentencing him to death within two months of his arrest."[42]

Until 2012, consensual sexual intercourse between men was a capital offense as well. After a change in the penal code, the "active person" can be punished with up to 100 lashes, while the passive person can still be sentenced to death. Men convicted of *lavat* (sodomy) typically receive more extreme punishment than women convicted of the same "crime." Women can be sentenced to 50 lashes for committing *mosahegheh* (lesbianism) for their first three convictions. If there is a fourth charge, then the punishment can be execution, although there are no confirmed reports of this taking place.

The legal distinctions for non-consensual acts are often vague, meaning that if someone is raped by a person of the same sex, they, too, may be convicted of a crime, although the punishment is less severe. Iran's volunteer paramilitary force, known as the *basij*, are known to entrap and intimidate people who are suspected of being gay, primarily men. Saba, a 32-year-old gay man, told Human Rights Watch that he and a friend were kidnapped by *basij* members, taken to an empty house, and raped before being returned to the street. During the assault, Saba said the man "kept telling me that if I cooperate with them they will not make trouble for us."[43]

Gays and lesbians are not just hounded by the state, but by their own families and society at large. Gay youths have been beaten and sexual assaulted by family members, especially in rural, poor, and less educated households. That's why most gay people in Iran refuse to disclose their sexual identity. Some marry women, but frequent male prostitutes.

In big cities, the situation is different. In Tehran, there is an active gay community and culture. This is especially true among middle- and upper-class Iranians who have the ability to create parallel lives, away from intolerant relatives and the prying eye of the state. There are gay couples who live together, and gay parties in private homes, where the hosts pay off the local morality police so that guests can come and go undisturbed. For the less affluent, there are certain parks known as hook-up spots.

The Internet provides the LGBTQ community a way to communicate. The government monitors and shuts down websites, but new gay dating sites and blogs crop up to replace them.

LGBTQ organizing in Iran is largely underground, but several international human rights groups provide aid, resources, and information to Iranians. One such organization is OutRight Action International, which does research and collects interviews with Iranian members of the community and distributes reports in both English and Farsi.[44] Another, the Iranian Railroad for Queer

Refugees, provides assistance to LGBTQ Iranians who want to leave the country and settle somewhere where they are safe.[45]

Thanks to the hard work of activists inside and outside the country, the government and society are becoming more tolerant. Young Iranians are more accepting, as are Iranians who travel abroad.

DOES THE GOVERNMENT REALLY SUBSIDIZE TRANSGENDER SURGERIES?

One of the remarkable contradictions is that the Iranian government encourages and helps transgender people to undergo sex reassignment surgery. This Islamic republic carries out more sex change operations than any other nation in the world, except for Thailand.

The remarkable transformation of the religious leaders from calling for transsexuals to be executed to helping them change their sex has been credited to the remarkable persistence of Maryam Khatoon Molkara, an Iranian woman who described herself as trapped in a male body.[46] In 1975, several years before the revolution, Molkara began a letter-writing campaign to Ayatollah Khomeini, seeking to convince him that Islam permitted gender reassignment. She had hopes that after the revolution, she would get her wish. Instead, she lost her job, was forcibly injected with male hormones, and institutionalized.

She didn't give up, though. Upon release, she was determined to meet Ayatollah Khomeini, who was then the nation's Supreme Leader. Wearing a man's suit, she approached his heavily guarded compound but was pounced upon by guards. Khomeini's brother, who had witnessed the scene, intervened and ushered her into the house. Granted an audience with Khomeini, Molkara pleaded for religious permission to get sex reassignment surgery. She left with a letter to the head of medical ethics giving her religious authorization to surgically change her gender.

Molkara ultimately got the operation in Thailand, but she returned to Iran to continue her campaign for transgender rights. In 1987, Khomeini issued a fatwa allowing sex reassignment and allowing transsexual women to live as women until they have surgery. The religious justification is that while the Quran bans homosexuality, it doesn't mention transsexuality. This has become the basis for the recognition of transgender people and for Iranian hospitals to carry out the operations. The government even subsidizes the procedures through state health insurance and housing support, and changes the person's identity documents to reflect the gender change.

Although at first glance the Iranian approach to transgender might seem remarkably liberal, it does have a negative side. Some people are pushed into operations they might not want. Many trans people simply wish to be accepted as they are—without surgery.

Also, the difference between being transgender and gay is not well understood in Iran, even within the medical profession, and there have been reports of gay men being pressured into surgery as a way of complying with the law. Some argue that the acceptance of sex-change procedures reinforces the strict gender divide that undermines the rights of the LGBTQ community.

While the government recognizes transgender people, they are still stigmatized in society at large. Families often reject transgender relatives, beating them and expelling them from the home. They may also face attacks from the police and religious fanatics, and discrimination at the workplace.

MEDEA BENJAMIN

HOW COMMONPLACE IS PROSTITUTION AND HOW ARE PROSTITUTES TREATED?

Prostitution is illegal in Iran and can yield heavy punishments, including prison sentences, up to 100 lashes, and even execution if the prostitute is a married woman. Despite the potential punishment and societal rejection, prostitution is widespread. The number of prostitutes is unknown, but in certain neighborhoods of Tehran, prostitutes can be seen hanging out on street corners (covered up, of course). One NGO estimates that there are about 10,000 female sex workers in Tehran alone.[47]

While prostitution is illegal, "sigheh," or temporary marriage, is permitted according to Shia law. Temporary marriage allows for short-term sexual relations, lasting from three days to many years. It is a private contract made in a verbal or written format, and it expires automatically without divorce. Sigheh is used in Iran as a legal cover for prostitution.

Most prostitutes are young—high school-age or younger—and have been recruited into the sex trade.[48] Some girls are runaways who fled abuse or were disowned by their conservative families. They connect with other runaways in communities known as *mahfels*, or safe havens, seeking liberation from societal suppression of youth culture and sexuality. Unfortunately, many of these *mahfels* also serve as entry points into sex rings where minors are vulnerable to recruitment by traffickers.

After sex workers age "past their prime" and leave the industry, many have sexually transmitted infections, injuries inflicted by clients, and other trauma that make it difficult for them to re-enter traditional society.

Recognizing the healthcare and psychological issues related to prostitution, the Ministry of Health has established drop-in centers and voluntary counseling/testing centers for female sex workers to get STD checks and medical treatment, as well as counseling.

WHY IS THERE SUCH A MAJOR DRUG PROBLEM IN IRAN?

With drug-related offenses making up the largest category of both prisoners and those executed in prison, there is obviously a big drug problem in Iran—and it's a problem that has been soaring out of control. In this, the U.S. and Iran are similar, both facing a national epidemic that affects young and old, rich and poor, secular and religious. In Iran, the hard drugs include crystal meth, heroin, synthetic hallucinogens, and opium trafficked from neighboring Afghanistan.[49] In 2016, the government estimated that 2.75 percent of the population was addicted (about 2.2 million people); the figure in the United States was 6.8 percent, or 21.6 million Americans. In Iran, those addicted are mostly men, but there are some women and even children who suffer from drug addiction.

One reason for Iran's drug problem is its geographical proximity to Afghanistan. Poppy, the source of opium and heroin, is transported from Afghanistan to Western Europe via Iran. Other socio-economic reasons include high unemployment and social frustration driven by sanctions and restraints imposed by the religious regime. The government has opened thousands of rehabilitation centers using methadone to wean addicts off drugs, and there are private rehab clinics as well.

While the government helps addicts get clean, it has a history of executing the drug dealers—even very small ones. So many Iranians have been hanged for drug offenses that it spurred a movement among elected officials and activists to abolish the death penalty for nonviolent drug-related offences.

In 2016, a year after over 500 people had been executed for drug offenses, human rights advocates succeeded in getting a majority of the nation's 290-seat Parliament to endorse a bill to end capital punishment for drug trafficking. This marked significant progress, as just the year before the same bill had only 70 supporters in Parliament.

In December 2017, President Houhani signed the bill and in January 2018, the law was ratified by the Guardian Council. According to the new law, only those distributing more than 50 kilograms of narcotics like opium, 2 kilograms of heroin or 3 kilograms of crystal meth will be sentenced to death. (Under the previous law, possessing 5kg of opium or 30g of herion was a capital offence.) There is no capital punishment for marijuana possession.

The new law is to be applied retrospectively, meaning that some 5,000 people awaiting execution for drug-related offenses are entitled to have their cases re-examined. This new law is considered a major step forward, but groups will continue pushing for an end to the death penalty for all non-lethal drug-related offenses, as required by international law.

IS ALCOHOL A PROBLEM IN THIS MUSLIM SOCIETY?

Alcohol has been illegal since the 1979 revolution and is taboo for devout Muslims. The Quran mentions the evils of wine but says nothing about drugs, so for a long time alcohol was seen as more dangerous than drugs. People caught drinking can be punished by 80 lashes.

Despite the ban, casual drinking is very commonplace, especially among young people at private parties. Before the revolution, the national drink was aragh sagi, which is distilled from raisins. It is still very popular.

Alcohol is relatively easy to buy. There is a vast, illegal distribution network with alcohol brought in from Iraqi Kurdistan. Dealers will deliver your order to your doorstep. But it is expensive, so many people resort to homemade brew, which is problematic because people can die from alcohol poisoning after consuming low-quality moonshine.

Iranians are said to be the third highest consumers of alcohol in Muslim-majority Middle Eastern countries, just after Lebanon and Turkey (both countries where it is legal to drink). Even official statistics show that at least 10 percent of the population uses alcohol. It is not casual drinking that is a problem, but alcoholism— and there are many alcoholics in Iran.

Previously, the government refused to admit there was an alcohol problem, but for the past several years, Alcoholics Anonymous groups have been allowed to function openly. In 2017, there were over 1,000 AA groups. In 2015, the Health Ministry took a further step in recognizing the problem of alcoholism by ordering drug addiction treatment centers to care for alcoholics. This is in marked contrast to the past. The government is slowly coming to the realization, in the case of drugs and alcohol, that you can't ignore or criminalize addiction out of existence, and that it is best handled by public health institutions and mutual aid groups, not by the criminal justice system.

*****

It is important to recognize that Iran is not a static society. Attitudes towards social issues are slowly evolving. Nowadays, there is more tolerance within society for gay rights, and more of a sense that people who have fallen on hard times, be it through prostitution, drugs, or alcohol, need help. As more activists get involved in these issues, hopefully they will be able to move those in power to embrace people with different sexual preferences and have more compassion for those who have fallen into hard times with drugs, alcohol, and prostitution.

CHAPTER 5: RELIGIOUS FREEDOM, FOR SOME

According to the government, an overwhelming 99.4 percent of Iranians are Muslims. Iranians must disclose their religious affiliation on official documents. Since the government does not recognize non-religious people, such as atheists or agnostics, most people—whether religious or not—formally identify as Muslim.

But there are religious minorities in this Shia-dominated country. There are Sunni Muslims and Muslims who practice Sufism. There are Christians, Zoroastrians, and Jews (groups the government considers "People of the Book"), and there are groups whose religions are not recognized, such as the Baha'is and Yarsan (Ahl-e Haq).

When Iran's President Rouhani addressed the United Nations in September 2017, he proclaimed that Iran, throughout its history, has been a bastion of tolerance for various religions and ethnicities: "We are the same people who rescued the Jews from Babylonian servitude, opened our arms to welcome Armenian Christians in our midst, and created the 'Iranian cultural continent' with a unique mix of diverse religions and ethnicities."

While it is true that Iran is open to some religious minorities, such as Christians, Zoroastrians, and Jews, they crack down on others, particularly the Baha'i. This chapter looks at the ways different religious groups are treated, as well as the fascinating paradox that in this theocratic Muslim state, most Iranians are just not very religious.

HOW DID SHIA ISLAM COME TO DOMINATE?

Before the Islamic conquest of Persia beginning in 637 A.D., Persians were mostly Zoroastrian, with a minority of Christians and Jews. When Islam was introduced by the Arab conquerors, the first to convert were the nobility and city dwellers. Slowly, the peasants also converted so that by the late 11th century, the majority of Persians had become Muslim. But over the centuries, they worked to create and preserve their own distinct version, maintaining their Persian language instead of using Arabic, and infusing their religious rituals with Persian culture.

There are two major strains of Islam, Shia and Sunni. Until the 16th century, most Persians adhered to the Sunni version of Islam. When the ruling Shah Ismail I ascended to power in 1501, he declared Shia Islam the official religion of the state. Those who refused to convert were murdered. The forced conversion continued for the next two centuries, until Iran became predominantly Shia.

Iran today is the largest Shia-dominated country in the world. Government figures show 90 percent of Iranian Muslims are Shia.

Within the Shia sect, there is a particular group called the Twelvers; Iranians are Twelvers, and about 80 percent of all Shia worldwide are Twelvers. Twelvers believe that there were 12 imams. They believe that the last one, Muhammad, is still alive and has been hiding in a cave for more than 1,000 years. They are waiting for him to come out, resume his rule, and establish a reign of peace and justice on earth.

The transformation of Iran into an overtly Shia state after the 1979 Islamic Revolution put Iran at the center of the Shia-Sunni split which dates back to the death of the Prophet Muhammad in 632 A.D. After the Prophet's death, most Muslims believed the new leader should be Abu Bakr, a friend of the Prophet and father of his wife Aisha. This group became known as the Sunnis and today make up about 80 percent of Muslims worldwide.

The minority of Muslims claimed the Prophet had anointed his cousin and son-in-law Ali to be his successor. They became known as Shia, a contraction of "shiaat Ali," or the partisans of Ali. The split deepened when Ali's son Imam Husayn was beheaded in 680 A.D. by Sunni troops. As time went on, the religious beliefs of the two groups became more and more divergent.

Saudi Arabia, home to the holiest Muslim sites of Mecca and Medina, is a Sunni state and considers itself the global center of Islam. Challenged by the Iranian revolution, Saudi rulers began to spread their Sunni version of Islam, Wahhabism, around the world. Both countries revived a centuries-old sectarian rivalry over the true interpretation of Islam. Much of the sectarian violence that has plagued the region can be traced to Saudi-Iranian rivalry.

HOW ARE SUNNI MUSLIMS TREATED?

While Sunni Muslims are the worldwide majority, in Iran they comprise roughly 10 percent of the Muslim population, and are a broad ethnic mix of Kurds, Arabs, Balochs, Persians, Pashtuns, Larestani, and Turkmens.[50] Most of them live in the country's border areas, although some have moved to the cities for more work opportunities. A more recent influx of Sunnis are refugees from Afghanistan.

The Sunnis face considerable persecution and discrimination, in large part because of the country's animosity towards the Sunni-majority Kingdom of Saudi Arabia.

Sunni Muslims do not have the same religious freedom as their Shia counterparts. Although about one million Sunnis live in Tehran, Iranian authorities will not allow them to build a single mosque in the capital city.[51] Officially, the government says that there are no Sunni mosques because Muslims should be united— all mosques are houses of God open to both Shia and Sunni. Some speculate, however, that the real reason is because the government is worried the mosques would be used by radicals to recruit youth who are frustrated with the Islamic Republic's ideology.[52] Authorities do allow small prayer houses for Sunni worship. Unlike mosques, prayers houses are often rental properties tucked away in residential neighborhoods, not prestigious buildings with minarets. The prayer houses usually don't have imams and staff, or religious instruction beyond prayer.

The teaching of Sunni ideology is banned in public schools. In private Sunni schools, the curriculum is regulated and administered by a government council that includes representatives of Iran's Shia Supreme Leader.[53] Sunnis also claim discrimination in employment, citing particular difficulty getting government jobs in the judicial and executive branches.[54]

In 2015, a prayer house in the Pounak neighborhood of western Tehran was raided and closed because, according to the government, the site was illegal and was being used to "recruit foreign citizens."[55]

Religious leaders within the Sunni community have been harassed, detained, arrested, and even executed for practicing their beliefs. At least 120 Sunnis were imprisoned for their faith as of 2016. In August 2016, 22 of them were executed after unfair trials that convicted them of *moharebeh*, which translates to "enmity towards God," and vague charges of involvement with terrorist activities.[56] Iranian authorities have refused to allow an investigation by a UN special rapporteur.

In October 2012, Sunni activists delivered a public letter to Iran's supreme leader, Ali Khamenei, to demand an end to discrimination.[57] The Sunni community welcomed the election of

President Rouhani in 2013 because his campaign included promises to address the discrimination, but very little has changed.

WHAT ABOUT SUFIS?

Sufis can be Shia or Sunni. Sufism is not a branch of Islam, but a practice that developed in the ninth and tenth centuries. Sufism in Iran has grown enormously since 1979. Before the revolution, about 100,000 people declared themselves Sufi Muslims. Today, there are somewhere between two and five million—making Iran the country with the largest Sufi population in the world.

Sufism has an ancient presence in Iran and is often associated with mysticism. It is considered the part of Islamic teaching that deals with the purification of self. Sufis strive to obtain the direct experience of God. Inspired by the mystics of Persian Zoroastrianism, Buddhism, Hinduism, and Christian monks, the early Sufis lived simple, ascetic lives in communal settings.

Sufism produced a flourishing intellectual culture. The most famous is the poet and Sufi master Jalal ad-Din Muhammad Rumi, known in Iran as Molavi. He was born in 1207 in a small village in what is now Afghanistan to Persian-speaking parents. He later traveled to Iran and Syria, ending up in Turkey, where he died in 1273. Rumi was a Sufi mystic who wrote thousands of poems, mostly love poems about the love he had for his mentor Shams of Tabriz, who disappeared three years after they met. Rumi incorporated poetry, music, and dance into religious practice, whirling while he meditated and composed poetry. In his honor, his followers founded the Order of the Whirling Dervishes. Rumi's work is recited, chanted, set to music, and used as inspiration for music, films, poems, and novels—and countless weddings. His peaceful and tolerant message appeals to people worldwide. Books of his writings have sold millions of copies and have been translated from the original Persian into 23 languages. Remarkably, after 800 years, Rumi is still one of the most popular poets, not only in Iran but worldwide.

In 2007, on the 800th anniversary of Rumi's birth, the Iranian government held an international ceremony and conference that was opened by the president. School bells throughout the country rang out on the day of his birth.

Similarly beloved and influential to modern Iranian culture is the 14th century poet Hafez. Like Rumi, Hafez was a Sufi Muslim, and books of his poetry are a fixture in Iranian homes—they are almost as common as the Quran. His home city of Shiraz is known today as Iran's most liberal city, due in part to the lasting influence of the ideas that Hafez expressed in his poetry. He targeted subjects including religious hypocrisy, writing, "Preachers who display their piety in prayer and pulpit behave differently when they're alone. Why do those who demand repentance do so little of it?"[58] Every day, Hafez's tomb in Shiraz is flocked by visitors who recite his poems and celebrate his life and work, keeping his 600-year-old critiques of religious conservatism alive and relevant.

After the revolution, Sufism became especially popular among women and young people. For many, it represents the embodiment of the true, tolerant, liberal Persian culture that is free of restrictions imposed by rigid clerics but also free of Western influence. In a country where playing music in public has been forbidden, music as part of Sufism is tolerated as a form of "alternative religious practice." In thousands of living rooms across the country, especially among the urban middle class, young men and women dance, sing, and recite Sufi-inspired poems.

Even President Rouhani, speaking before the United Nations in 2017, praised Iran's poets as the way Iran has spread its influence—as opposed to military conquest: "Our ambassadors are our poets, our mystics, and our philosophers. We have reached the shores of this side of the Atlantic through Rumi, and spread our influence throughout Asia with Saadi. We have already captured with Hafez."[59]

But the revolution has had a checkered relationship with Sufis. While for the most part, Sufis are tolerated by the government, some traditional clerics see Sufism as a threat. They understand that Sufism became so popular, in part, as a form of opposition to political and state Islam.

Sufi leaders who are critical of the government have been arrested and convicted of vague crimes like "disturbing public order" and "taking action against national security."[60] Sufi centers of worship have been targeted by authorities. In 2006, a Sufi meeting house in Qom was torn down by the political militia known as the Basij, and the approximately 1,200 Sufis who were trying to defend the structure were arrested. In 2007, another Sufi worship space in Borujerd was burned down. When some Sufis expressed their support for the dissident Green Movement in 2009, the government crackdown intensified. Iranian authorities used bulldozers to destroy a Sufi prayer house and the mausoleum of the 19th century Sufi poet Nasir Ali in the city of Isfahan.

In May 2014, approximately 35 Sufis were convicted on charges related to their religious activities and given sentences ranging from three months to four years in prison. Another 10 Sufi activists were either serving prison terms or had cases pending against them.[61]

WHICH NON-MUSLIM GROUPS ARE GRANTED THE RIGHT TO WORSHIP?

As discussed above, Iran is a Shia Muslim state that discriminates against Sunni Muslims and sometimes frowns upon those who practice Sufism. But how are non-Muslims treated?

In sharp contrast to Saudi Arabia, where it is illegal to openly practice a religion other than Islam, the Iranian government recognizes Christians, Zoroastrians, and Jews as "People of the Book." These groups are allowed to openly practice their religion and their freedom to worship is enshrined within the Iranian constitution.[62] They are also granted representation in Parliament, with two seats reserved for Armenian Christians, one for Assyrian and Chaldean Christians, one for Jews, and one for Zoroastrians.[63]

The size of the Christian population is difficult to pin down, with estimates ranging from 270,000–500,000. Most are Armenians and Assyrians.[64] There are about 600 churches in Iran. Christians living in Iran are allowed to drink alcohol and eat pork, even though they are forbidden substances for the majority of Iranians.

Christians are fully integrated into Iranian society. Famous members of Iran's Christian community include the captain of the national football team Andranik Teymourian, well-loved musician Loris Tjeknavorian, and Sombat Hacoupian, who started a men's clothing brand that has become a household name.

Not all Christians, however, are well received by the authorities. Iranians who were not born Christians but converted from Islam face discrimination. Converts may find themselves charged with crimes both secular and religious in nature. Iranian authorities have raided church services and threatened religious leaders who they suspect are involved in proselytizing. Some reports indicate that in 2016, there were about 90 Christians in prison, both converts and people accused of proselytizing. One case is that of Yousef Nadarkhani,[65] a pastor who, in 2009, questioned Islam's monopoly on education. Charged with apostasy (abandoning Islam) and evangelizing Muslims, he was originally sentenced to death. After an international outcry, he was released in 2012.

The second "recognized" minority religion is Zoroastrianism. Zoroastrians have a long history in the region, and they are the oldest surviving religious community in Iran. Founded by the Prophet Zoroaster, it is one of the oldest monotheistic religions. Zoroastrians believe that the god Ahura Mazda, which translates to Wise Lord, created the world and that fire represents the God's wisdom and light. Zoroastrianism not only preceded but is also thought to have influenced the beliefs of the major Abrahamic religions, such as the belief in heaven, hell, and a messianic figure. A 2011 census documented only 25,000 Zoroastrians in Iran, although members of the religious community argue that the number is larger.[66] There is much goodwill among the general population toward Zoroastrianism. Many Muslim Iranians wear a necklace with Faravahar, a Zoroastrian symbol that represents the religion's basic principles: good thoughts, good words, good deeds.

The third officially sanctioned minority religion is Judaism. The Jewish community in Iran is small—about 10,000–20,000. (There are many more Iranian Jews, about 200,000, who live in Israel.) Nevertheless, Jews living in Iran constitute the largest Jewish community in the Middle East outside Israel and the second largest Jewish community in a predominantly Muslim country (Turkey is the first).[67] Prior to the Iranian Revolution, the number of Jews was roughly 80,000, but most fled the country and resettled elsewhere.[68] Many of those who stayed behind claim that while the government is anti-Israel, it is not against Jews. In Tehran alone, there are more than 10 kosher butcher stores, five kosher restaurants, and five Jewish schools.[69] In 2016, the seat in Parliament reserved for a member of the Jewish community was held by a surgeon named Ciamak Morsadegh. Morsadegh claimed that there are about 60 synagogues in Iran and that, unlike some

European countries where synagogues must be guarded from attacks, Jews in Iran felt secure and faced no such threats.[70]

But Iran's standing with the country's Jewish community was badly tarnished under the 2005–2013 presidency of Mahmoud Ahmadinejad, who became infamous internationally for statements denying or downplaying the scale of the Holocaust. His successor Rouhani tried to undo the damage.

On his first visit to the UN General Assembly in New York in 2013, Rouhani was accompanied by Iran's Jewish member of Parliament. Rouhani called the Holocaust a crime against humanity and has been very careful to note that he is a critic of the Israeli government, not the Jewish people. In September 2013, on Rosh Hashanah, the Jewish new year, he made headlines globally by tweeting: "As the sun is about to set here in #Tehran I wish all Jews, especially Iranian Jews, a blessed Rosh Hashanah." The tweet was accompanied by a photo of an Iranian Jew praying at a synagogue in Tehran. Rouhani's government also showed support by donating half a million dollars to Tehran's Jewish hospital.[71]

Anti-Jewish sentiment, however, is still present. Some high-ranking clerics continue to preach anti-Semitic messages and the state has targeted individuals believed to have connections with Israel.[72] But among the public, there is widespread sympathy for Jews. According to a 2014 poll by the U.S.-based Anti-Defamation League, Iranians—who have been accustomed to "Death to Israel" rallies since the time of the revolution—are the most pro-Jewish people in the Middle East (with the exclusion of Israel). In the same poll, when asked if Jews "still talk too much about what happened to them in the Holocaust," only 18 percent of Iranians agreed, compared to 22 percent of Americans.[73]

WHY ARE THE BAHA'I DISCRIMINATED AGAINST?

In contrast to the recognized minority religions are those, such as the Baha'is and Yarsan (Ahl-e Haq), that are not recognized by the state.

The Baha'i are the largest non-Muslim minority in Iran, with a population estimated at 300,000 (and about 6 million worldwide). The Baha'i faith was founded in Iran in the 19th century by its prophet, Baha'u'llah. Iran banned the faith in 1981, soon after the Islamic Revolution.

The Islamic Republic considers the Baha'i faith heretical because it was founded after the death of the Prophet Muhammad, who is perceived in Islam as the final prophet. Former Iranian president Ayatollah Akbar Hashemi Rafsanjani called the Baha'i faith a "deviant sect created by colonialists who we have always and will always oppose." The Iranian regime's typical accusation is that the Baha'i faith is a foreign plot and Baha'is are "agents of Israel and America."[74]

UN officials stated that the Baha'i community is the "most severely persecuted religious minority" in Iran because the multiple forms of discrimination "affect their enjoyment of economic, social and cultural rights."[75] The Iranian Revolutionary Guard and their supporters have demolished or desecrated Baha'i cemeteries and holy places, and confiscated community property.[76] Legally, Baha'is are not even allowed to leave property to their heirs. Hate speech and hate crimes against them are common.

Baha'is are barred from pursuing military careers and face prejudice in many other fields of employment and education. Iranian authorities have seized Baha'i-owned businesses and detained Baha'i students who challenge their lack of access to equal education and employment. In 2014, the government demolished the Baha'i cemetery in Shiraz, where many of the victims are buried.[77]

Leaders of the Baha'i faith are commonly targeted. Scores of Baha'is have been imprisoned for peacefully practicing their religion, with vague charges of threatening national security.

Detained Baha'is have reported torture, such as the alleged torture of 24 Baha'is in Golestan Province in 2016, but the accusations are rarely investigated.[78] Worst of all, Iranian officials have executed more than 200 Baha'i leaders since the revolution in 1979. According to the Center for Human Rights in Iran, more than 80 Baha'is are currently being held in Iranian prisons.[79]

A group known as the "Baha'i 7" were arrested in 2008, charged with "espionage for Israel, insulting religious sanctities and propaganda against the system" and sentenced to 20 years in prison. Amnesty International considered them prisoners of conscience. There is hope that they will be released from their 20-year sentences due to a change in Iran's penal code that allows sentences to be carried out cumulatively instead of consecutively.[80]

Due to this persecution, since 1999 the U.S. government's Commission on International Religious Freedoms has annually labeled Iran as a Country of Particular Concern due to its "systematic, ongoing, and egregious violations of religious freedom, including prolonged detention, torture, and executions based primarily or entirely upon the religion of the accused."[81]

WHAT ABOUT THE OTHER NON-RECOGNIZED RELIGION KNOWN AS YARSAN, OR AHL-E-HAQ?

Yarsan, or Ahl-e-Haq, meaning People of Truth, is a religious minority mostly residing in the Kurdish-dominated province of Kermanshah in the northwest of Iran. The faith also has followers in Iraq and Turkey. Yarsan is a syncretic religion that dates back to the 14th century. Until the 20th century, it was strictly for Kurds who were born into it. Their beliefs include the transmigration of the soul and that human beings go through a cycle of 1001 incarnations, during which they may become more purified based on their actions.

The government of Iran considers this religion a "false cult." Yarsan believers say that the government tries to convert their community to Islam, imprisons their leaders, and violates the social, cultural, and economic rights of its followers.

ARE THERE ATHEISTS IN IRAN?

Certainly there are many atheists in Iran, but there is no way of knowing how many. Iran is one of 13 countries where atheists could be given the death penalty, but this is not enforced. Atheists who don't speak out publicly to advocate their views have no problems. There are even several pro-atheist Facebook groups that poke fun at religious figures, but people participate anonymously.

In an online chat about Iranians and religion, someone wrote, "I am an atheist and an Iranian. I am also anonymous, which speaks volumes." Another Iranian responded differently: "I was raised in Iran in a non-practicing Muslim family and became an atheist when I was around 14. I have never felt any reason to hide it. Some people are surprised if I tell them I don't believe in God, but nobody has ever bothered me and I've never felt intimidated."

CAN MUSLIMS CHANGE THEIR RELIGION?

In Iran, it's a crime for a Muslim to convert to another religion— once born a Muslim, you must remain a Muslim. The act of changing or denouncing your faith, known as apostasy, is a capital offense. It has been decades since anyone was executed for apostasy; the last known case was someone who converted to Christianity in 1990.[82]

Still, anyone converting to another religion tends to do so quietly to avoid government retaliation.

ARE IRANIANS MUSLIMS VERY RELIGIOUS?

One of the fascinating idiosyncrasies of Iran is that while it is a theocratic Muslim state, most Iranians are not particularly religious.

The ruling regime insists that it has created a more religious society since the 1979 revolution, and certainly people are inculcated with a heavy dose of religion in school and through the state-run media. Women must dress according to religious dictates. In the holy month of Ramadan, people cannot eat or drink (even water) in public. When mosques issue their five daily calls to prayer, the call resonates throughout the neighborhoods on loud, outdoor speakers. By law, all public buildings must have prayer rooms.

Yet at office buildings, shopping malls, and bus stations, you see few people praying. In contrast to Saudi Arabia, where workplaces are forced to close for prayer, most Iranian businesses stay open during prayer time.

Polls show that most Iranians say religion is an important part of their daily lives.[83] But with a government that insists on imposing religiosity, many Iranians have rebelled by becoming less and less religious in the traditional sense. Clerics can impose their beliefs on many aspects of Iranian life, but they can't force people to be believers.

CHAPTER 6: THE PARADOXICAL STATUS OF IRANIAN WOMEN

Two key societal restrictions affect the lives of Iranian women: patriarchal values that pre-date the 1979 revolution, and post-1979 institutional structures based on hardline interpretations of Islamic principles. Both influences see women mainly through the lens of wives and mothers, and use this narrow view as a pretext for restricting women's public and private lives. While the restrictions affect all women in some fashion, they are far more pronounced among women who are poor, rural, and/or religious than they are among women who are middle class, educated, urban, and secular.

On the other hand, Westerners who think of Iranian women as passive, hijab-clad individuals relegated to the confines of their homes are quite misinformed. Yes, Iranian women are oppressed—the country ranks 139 out of 145 on the World Economic Forum's 2016 Global Gender Gap report[84]—and the mandatory dress code of the hijab is a visible sign of government interference in their lives. Nevertheless, Iranian women enjoy far greater freedom than women in many other countries in the region, particularly Saudi Arabia, where women live under a much stricter male guardianship system. In Afghanistan, many women remain illiterate and confined to their homes. In striking contrast, Iranian women are well educated, involved in all aspects of society, and are powerful agents of change who continuously fight for their rights, even at great personal risk.

WHAT WERE WOMEN'S RIGHTS UNDER THE SHAH?

While the Pahlavi dynasty (1925–1979) was fraught with repression and corruption, the penchant for Western modernization, coupled with pressure by Iranian women, led to fundamental gains for women. A national referendum in 1963 granted women the right to vote and to run for public office. A woman was promoted to a cabinet position, Minister of Education, in 1968, and in 1969 five female judges were appointed, including future Nobel prize winner Shirin Ebadi.

The Women's Organization of Iran was founded in 1966 to promote women's rights. One of its major victories was the Family Protection Act, enacted in 1967, and updated in 1975. Despite vociferous objections by religious and conservative communities, it gave Iranian women the right to divorce their husbands, object to their husbands' polygamy, and contest their children's custody after divorce. It also raised the minimum age for girls to marry from 13 years to 18 years. In a major breakthrough for women in the region, abortion was legalized.

Immediately after the 1979 Revolution, women lost many of the rights they had achieved. The Family Protection Act was repealed because Supreme Leader Ayatollah Khomeini considered it in violation of Islam and sharia law.

WHAT IS THE NORM TODAY IN TERMS OF MARRIAGE?

Since the beginning of the 20th century, Iran has generally been a monogamous society. Legally, Iranian men can have up to four wives, but polygamy is uncommon and exists mostly among the religious elite.[85]

After the revolution, the marriage age for girls was reduced from 15 years to "puberty," which is nine under Islamic law. In 2002, it was raised to 13, but the girl's father can ask the court for permission to marry off his daughter below this age.[86]

Child marriages can be found among conservative, rural families, as well as poor, women-headed households and families with drug problems. The norm, however, is for Iranians to get married later in life. The average marriage age in 2016 was 24 for women and 27 for men, and even at that age, almost half the young people remain unmarried.[87]

The low marriage rate is attributed to the deterioration of the economy, and the increased opportunities for romantic relationships outside of marriage. Many couples, especially in the big cities, cohabitate without getting married, a practice known as white marriage. Educated, independent women also complain that it is difficult to find open-minded Iranian men who appreciate liberated women.[88]

Arranged marriages do still exist, but mostly in the rural areas. These days, the Internet has become key to matchmaking. Using websites similar to Match.com or e-Harmony, young, urban Iranians find their mates for a lifetime, or for a night. The government tries to crack down on dating sites it considers immoral, but as soon as one site gets blocked, another appears. Finally admitting defeat and following the adage "if you can't beat 'em, join 'em," the government started its own official "spouse-finding" website in 2015, which is mostly used by religious youth. Other, more liberal sites still abound, especially in Tehran, where there is even an app for gay and lesbian singles.[89]

HOW COMMON IS DIVORCE?

A major gain that women had made before the 1979 revolution was the equal right to divorce. One of the revolutionary government's first acts was not only to suspend the Family Protection Act but also to dismantle Family Courts. Men were given the freedom to divorce their wives by simple declaration, and gained exclusive custody of the children. Mothers might be granted custody until the children are seven, but then custody reverts back to the fathers. Even if the father dies, custody does not revert to the mother but to the child's paternal grandfather.

If the husband is unwilling to divorce, the wife must prove that he is abusive, has psychological problems, or is somehow unable to uphold his marital responsibilities.

Divorce is frowned upon by the state and is often considered shameful by the community, particularly in the more conservative parts of the country. It can leave women in a difficult financial and social situation.

Despite the obstacles, the divorce rate in Iran is high. In 2014, about 20 percent of marriages ended in divorce, a statistic decried by the clerics as an affront to the values of the Islamic Republic.[90] Reasons for divorce include adultery, drug addiction, physical abuse, in-law interference, impotence, women's greater financial independence, and greater societal acceptance in more educated, urban households. Conservatives blame it on "growing godlessness" among the youth and the corrupting influences of the West.

IS ABORTION LEGAL?

Among the policies that Iranian women fought for and won during the Shah's time was the 1977 legalization of abortion, which was extremely rare in the Middle East. This changed with the 1979 revolution, however, when the clerics cited the Quran's condemnation of infanticide as the reason to prohibit abortions. Over time, the rules have been slightly loosened to make abortion legal in the case of an abnormal fetus or if the mother's life is in danger.

Otherwise, abortion is forbidden, and those providing or receiving an illegal abortion can be severely punished with a prison term of three to ten years.[91]

But illegal or induced abortions still occur every day, with an estimated 120,000 illegal abortions performed every year.[92] Gynecologists report that illegal, black market abortions have had a terrible impact on women's health.

HOW MANY CHILDREN DO WOMEN HAVE?

At the start of the revolution, Ayatollah Khomeini opposed the Shah's family planning clinics, insisting that birth control was a Western plot to have fewer Muslims in the world. He ordered the destruction of all family planning clinics. The birth rate soared from 2.1 to 4.2, among the highest in the world.

Even the Supreme Leader realized that the growth rate was too much for the country to bear and had to be lowered. The family planning clinics were reopened, and the nation's birth control program of free condoms, vasectomies, pills, and family planning education became a model worldwide—except for the prohibition on abortion.

The push to lower the birthrate was so successful that by 2012, it had plummeted to just 1.7, the lowest in the region. The government now had the opposite concern—that Iran would become a nation of old people. So, at a time when environmentalists are concerned that the global population will surpass eight billion by 2030 (by some calculations, human overpopulation may have occurred at four billion people), Iran switched course once again, setting a goal of doubling the nation's population from 80 million to 150 million by 2050.

To achieve this goal, the government took some steps that were helpful to families, such as increasing maternity leave from six months to a full nine months (compared to three months in the United States) and allowing a two-week leave for fathers. Other measures had a markedly negative impact on women: canceling subsidies for condoms and birth control pills; eliminating free vasectomies; making divorce harder (couples now have to go to counseling first). During President Ahmadinejad's last year in office, the government eliminated the budget for family planning, thus ending one of the most successful programs of its kind in the world.[93]

WHAT IS THE DRESS CODE FOR WOMEN?

For the last 100 years, women's dress in Iran has been an arena of struggle between the government, clergy, men, and women themselves. That's why women's clothing, particularly the veil, is as much a political symbol as a religious one.

During the beginning of the 20th century, most women were isolated in their homes and concealed in public by long chadors, a loose and usually dark-colored cloth that covers the head and body but leaves the face visible. When Reza Shah Pahlavi rose to power in 1925, he pushed a process of modernization and secularization, including encouraging women to adopt Western dress. In 1936, he went even further, issuing a royal decree declaring it illegal for women to wear the traditional chador. Most upper class and educated women happily adopted more Western-styled clothing and shed their chadors, but the decision to ban the veil was vehemently opposed by the clerics and religious women.

Women who chose Islamic dress were harassed by police, and their veils forcibly removed. As a result, rather than appear in public in an "immodest" fashion, religious women often remained at home, either by their choice or at their family's insistence. This meant that fewer religious women were educated or employed outside the home.

Resistance to the ban was so strong that when Mohammed Reza Pahlavi took over from his father in 1941, the ban was lifted. As the Shah's pro-Western government became increasingly repressive, more and more women, including liberal university students, began wearing the headscarf and chador as a symbol of opposition. Many middle and upper class women started wearing the chador to demonstrations as a way so show solidarity with poor women, who were traditionally more religious. Ironically, the veil became a symbol of liberation from the dictatorial state. Little did the women realize that the new government ushered in by the revolution would soon make Islamic dress mandatory.

Once in power, the Supreme Leader called for a return to modesty and Islamic dress, but the government assured women that this was only a recommendation.[94] Then, in 1980, the veil became mandatory in government and public offices, and in 1983 it became mandatory for all women. Women took to the streets in protest on many occasions, but were unsuccessful, leaving them with a profound sense of betrayal.

According to law, women must cover their entire body except for their faces and hands; women who do not wear the chador must wear a long overcoat called a manteau. The manteau is supposed to be loose fitting and thick enough to conceal the clothes underneath. Women are not supposed to wear brightly colored clothes or clothes designed to attract men's attention.

The pendulum had swung to the other side. Now, women who were *not* veiled faced harassment by authorities. *Bad hijab* became a crime and was defined not just by an uncovered head, but also uncovered arms and legs; tight, bright or see-through clothes; clothing with foreign words; makeup; and even nail polish. The punishment in the 1983 Penal Law was 74 lashes, which was changed in 1996 to a prison sentence of up to four months and a monetary fine. Over the years, the rules have been relaxed, with women merely issued a warning.

Some women believe that the dress code liberates them from worrying about their appearance and allows them to focus on more important issues, such as education and employment. Others condemn the practice of forced veiling as repressing their rights of expression and bodily autonomy.

In 2013, the newly elected President Rouhani took a stand, albeit a small one, against the strict adherence to the Islamic dress code favored by his predecessors. Rouhani stated, "If a woman or a man does not comply with our rules for clothing, his or her virtue should not come under question ... In my view, many women in our society who do not respect our hijab laws are virtuous. Our emphasis should be on the virtue."[95] His remarks provoked a critical response from Ayatollah Khamenei and other members of the clergy.

While in pre-revolutionary times women rebelled by wearing the veil, today Iranian women rebel by wearing colorful scarves pushed back to expose as much hair as they can get away with, tight-fitting manteaus, and gobs of makeup. Makeup has become a symbol of defiance, and Iran is the second largest market for cosmetics in the Middle East, right behind Saudi Arabia.[96]

Women who test the boundaries of modesty take a personal risk. As in other Islamic countries, such as Saudi Arabia, Sudan, and Malaysia, Iran has a police force tasked with enforcing the dress code. Iran's morality police, *Gasht-e Ershad*, are constantly on the lookout for "immoral behavior." In 2014, a group of youth released a video of themselves, including women without head scarves, joyfully dancing to Pharrell William's popular song "Happy." The individuals in the video were later arrested and charged with "hurting public chastity." They were sentenced to a year in prison and 91 lashes, but thanks to a fierce international outcry, their sentence was suspended.[97]

While the morality police used to be empowered to impose fines or arrest transgressors, as of 2016 the nation's 7,000-strong force, which includes women, is only supposed to issue warnings to adjust or remove the insulting attire or to report violations to the police, who then decide whether to take action.[98] But that is not always the case, and in some instances the morality police turn violent. In February 2017, a 14-year-old girl was beaten and detained for wearing ripped jeans in public.[99]

Facebook groups such as "My Stealthy Freedom," have popped up with women challenging the dress code by posting photos of themselves unveiled in public places.[100] An initiative started in 2017 by Masih Alinejad, who lives in the United States, used the hashtag #whitewednesdays. It encouraged women to post pictures and videos of themselves wearing white headscarves as symbols of protest, and—if they dared—to take off their headscarves while walking in public.[101] According to Alinejad, in the first two weeks, hundreds of women had already submitted videos, some of which had 500,000 views. One participant said she took the risk because "even if this leads me to jail and sleeping with cockroaches, it would be worth it to help the next generation."

IS IRAN REALLY THE NOSE JOB CAPITAL OF THE WORLD?

One of the most ironic ways that Iranian women snub their noses at the modesty-obsessed clerics is by getting nose jobs. Iran has become the nose job capital of the world, with over 70,000 rhinoplasty operations every year.[102] The women—and increasingly men as well—don't try to hide their surgeries. Going out on the street with a bandaged nose has become a status symbol.

Iranian women also challenge Islamic codes of modesty by obtaining cosmetic surgeries such as liposuction to improve their figures, eyebrow tattoos, botox injections in their cheeks, and collagen in their lips to make them fuller. The public is bombarded with advertisements flaunting photos of clients before and after plastic surgery.

For a group of young women I met on the streets of Tehran, their obsession with their appearance—nose jobs, full lips, lots of makeup, dyed-blonde hair sticking out from the loose-fitting, colorful scarves—definitely represented a form of protest. "The government forces us to cover our heads and our bodies, so we use our faces to display our beauty," smiled a 20-year-old student as she puffed on a cigarette in a Tehran cafe lined with photos of American movie stars. When I asked if she was afraid the morality police would punish her for wearing tight clothes and so much makeup, she laughed. "We just run away from them."

WHAT ACCESS TO EDUCATION DO WOMEN HAVE?

Throughout the first half of the 20th century, there was a slow but steady expansion of women's education. In 1935, the University of Tehran admitted female students to the institution for the first time, and in the ensuing decades, higher education for women became a norm among upper class Iranians.[103]

Education for girls became universal and compulsory in 1944. Primary education, which lasts until ninth grade, is provided free through public schools.[104] High school is not compulsory but is free. Iran boasts that the literacy rate for women and girls between the ages of 15 and 24 is virtually universal, 99 percent.[105]

But the 1979 revolution has had a devastating impact on the quality of girls' education. Coeducation was banned by religious authorities, causing many schools to close their doors to girls. In all-girls schools, the curriculum was often designed by religious leaders to promote gendered career paths, such as running households or working in hospitals.[106] The new regime codified this gendered division of labor by forbidding certain majors. Women were not allowed to study law, and men were not permitted to enroll in studies deemed feminine.[107] Scholarships to study abroad were not available to unmarried women, as the state feared that the women would be negatively affected by foreign influences.[108]

Women pushed for equal educational opportunities, and during the reform period of President Khatami from 1997–2005, many of these restrictions were lifted. In the early 2000s, women's enrollment in university began to surpass the number of male students, and unmarried women were granted the opportunity to pursue scholarships for study abroad, although they still require permission from their fathers.[109]

When Mahmoud Ahmadinejad was elected president in 2005, however, women's gains in education were reversed, as authorities blamed women's education for too much competition in the job market, a rising divorce rate, and the declining fertility rate.[110]

Bans and quotas to cap the number of women were placed on certain majors, and women were only allowed to attend institutions of higher education within their hometowns.[111] Many universities also had gender segregation policies that required separate classes for men and women.

Women hoped to see new education reforms when Hassan Rouhani became president in 2013—during his campaign he directly criticized the university gender quotas that limited the percentage of women.[112] As of 2017, gender-based quotas on admissions and fields of study remain common in Iranian universities, especially since the practice is supported by Supreme Leader Khamenei.[113]

The effects of the backlash on women's education during Ahmadinejad's time and Rouhani's inability to bring about major change led to a decline in the number of Iranian women obtaining higher education. In 2007, 62 percent of students entering university were women. By 2013 that number had plummeted to 48.2 percent, but in ensuing years it once again rose to over 50 percent.[114]

WHAT WORK OPTIONS ARE OPEN FOR WOMEN?

Women are permitted to work in Iran, but there are countless barriers to the type of careers they can pursue, and religious authorities strongly encourage women to stay home to fulfill the traditional roles of wives and mothers. Despite being over 50 percent of university graduates, women only make up 17 percent of the official labor market. Over one-third of university-education women are unemployed.[115]

While many women choose not to enter the job market due to social pressure, unemployment among women willing to work is at least twice as high as the rate for men.[116]

The government formally prohibits discrimination on the basis of gender in the workplace, but the limits placed on women's education and the social/cultural bias towards men in the hiring process combine to result in far fewer professional options for women.[117] In occupations where both men and women compete for the same positions, women in Iran—as in most of the world—are less likely to be hired. Female workers are often paid less than their male counterparts, especially in factories.[118] In the legal arena, women can train as judges, but they can only become assistant judges.

Economic sanctions imposed by the international community have also had a negative impact on women's employment opportunities. The disrupted economy creates more competition between men and women, and in the case of layoffs, women are much more likely to lose their jobs than men.

Women's employment possibilities can also be limited by their families. Although Iran does not have a strict guardianship policy like Saudi Arabia, where men have decision-making power over key aspects of women's lives, some Iranian employers require permission from the father or husband. The husband or father also has the ability to prohibit travel—their permission is needed for a visa application. This can prevent women from being employed in positions where travel is likely. Policies that began in 2014 encouraging women to have more children to reverse the nation's declining fertility rate made it even more difficult for women to find and retain employment, since employers are biased against women who take time off for childcare.

Women had hoped that President Rouhani would address discrimination in the workforce when he came to power in 2013. In July 2016, he temporarily suspended hiring in government agencies that discriminated against women, but the effort produced limited improvements.[119] As in other areas of reform, Rouhani's efforts were slow and halfhearted in the face of opposition from hardliners within the government and religious sector.

Despite all these limitations, many women still thrive in their professions. Iranian women are doctors, lawyers, journalists, engineers, professors, artists, and even truck drivers. Many run their own businesses. The Association of Iranian Business Women lists women-run businesses that range from architectural firms to medical production facilities to family farms.

CAN WOMEN VOTE, RUN FOR OFFICE, AND HOLD POSITIONS OF POWER?

Iranian women secured the right to vote and run for public office in 1963, although these rights were strongly opposed by conservative clerics. That same year, six women were elected to the Iranian Parliament. By 1978, just prior to the Islamic Revolution, there were 22 female members of Parliament.[120]

In the first parliamentary election after the Islamic Revolution, only four women won and many women who had occupied powerful positions, such as judges, were demoted or dismissed. Women's representation in government has remained minimal, with minor ebbs and flows. Some of the greatest gains were under the reform leadership of President Khatami, when record numbers of women were put in senior advisory government positions.

Undeterred by the low odds of winning, women still actively participate in politics and run for office. In 2008, 585 women campaigned for elected office (out of 7,168 total candidates), but only nine were elected.[121]

There has been a raging debate about whether it is legal for women to run for president. Article 115 of the constitution states that the president must be chosen from among the "religious and political *rijal*." The debate revolves around the definition of the word *rijal*. Some insist on the literal Arab translation, which means men. Others, including former President Rafsanjani, argue that in the constitutional context, it simply means "person" and therefore can be a woman.[122]

So far, the male definition has prevailed. In 2009, 42 women attempted to run for president, but all were disqualified by the Guardian Council. In 2013, all 30 women who attempted to get on the presidential ballot were disqualified.[123] In 2017, the highest number of women ever, 137, attempted to run, but all were banned.[124]

In Parliament, however, 17 women were elected to the 290-member body—the highest number since the revolution. This was particularly significant because for the first time, women had more members in Parliament than the clerics, who had only 16 seats.[125]

Still, Iranian women ranked near the bottom in a worldwide comparison of parliaments, placing 178 out of 193 in 2017.[126] Nevertheless, the shift toward electing more women, combined with the declining number of conservative hardliners winning seats in Parliament, is promising. A campaign called "Changing the male face of Parliament" is working toward a goal of 30 percent women by the 2020 election.[127]

CAN IRANIAN WOMEN PLAY SPORTS AND ATTEND SPORTING EVENTS?

Prior to the 1979 revolution, female athletes were encouraged to participate in national and international competitions. Participation declined in the 1980s, but since then there has been a steady increase in women's involvement in both individual and team sports, including soccer, hockey, rugby, volleyball, and even chess. Men are not allowed to attend women's competitions.

Being an athlete offers opportunities for Iranian women to travel abroad, but women do require permission from a male relative, such as a father or husband. Soccer team captain and champion player Niloufar Ardalan couldn't attend the Asian Football Confederation's women's championship in 2015 because her husband wouldn't grant her permission to travel to Malaysia.[128]

Sometimes Iranian athletes face discrimination from international hosts. In 2011, the soccer association FIFA disqualified the Iranian soccer team from the Olympic competition, saying the scarves their government obliged them to wear was a breach of the association's dress code.

Iranian women are also struggling for the right to attend sporting events where males are playing. Iranians share the world's love of volleyball and soccer, but women have been barred from attending. The authorities have justified the ban by insisting that there is a lack of proper infrastructure for women, including bathrooms, and that men used profanities and can become violent.

One famous act of protest was the 1997 "football revolution" when about 5,000 women defied the ban and stormed the gates of the stadium to celebrate the national football team's qualifying for the World Cup.

In 2006, a comical Iranian film called "Offside" portrayed young women sneaking into a World Cup qualifying match. Shot in Iran and inspired by the director's daughter, who did sneak into stadiums, the film received international acclaim but was banned from being shown inside Iran.

The struggle achieved international notoriety in June 2014 when a British-Iranian student, Ghonchech Ghavami, tried to attend a men's volleyball match. She was imprisoned for 100 days, much of the time in solitary confinement.[129] In 2015, the Deputy Minister for Sports announced that women would be permitted to attend some male sporting events. Volleyball, basketball, handball, and tennis matches were opened because they were considered less rowdy, but not soccer or wrestling.

A group of young women started a campaign called Open Stadiums, which identifies itself as "a movement of Iranian women seeking to end discrimination and let women attend stadiums." Prominent male athletes and coaches have called for the ban to be lifted.

In September 2017, the absurdity of the ban was evident at a World Cup qualifying match in Tehran between Iran and Syria. Syrian women were allowed into the stadium to cheer their team while Iranian women left outside, protesting. This led a number of female members of Parliament to condemn the ban.

While Iranians keep pushing from the inside, pressure is also coming from outside the country, including from the international soccer and volleyball federations that threaten to censure Iran if the restrictions on women are not lifted.[130]

HOW SEGREGATED ARE PUBLIC SPACES?

Iran is not as gender segregated as Saudi Arabia, where all the schools, public spaces, and even private businesses like McDonald's are segregated. Public places such as beaches or swimming pools are segregated in Iran, but businesses, parks, and government buildings are not. Perhaps the most segregated space is the mosque, where women are physically partitioned away from men.

Buses are integrated, but there are seats reserved for women, usually in the back. Women can be taxi drivers, but they can only pick up other women. In the Tehran metro, the first and last cars are usually reserved for women. While these cars are marked "Women Only," that doesn't mean women have to ride exclusively in those cars. They can ride in the middle cars with men, but women often choose the segregated cars for safety and security.

HOW COMMON IS VIOLENCE AGAINST WOMEN?

Violence against women is commonplace—domestic violence as well as street harassment and sexual harassment in the workplace. Violence against women is especially prevalent in poor, rural families, where traditional male domination is greater and women have few alternatives. Women in prison are also subjected to sexual violence.

Victims are usually afraid to report the abuses, and government authorities refuse to acknowledge the scale of the problem. In 2014, the country was shocked by a wave of acid attacks in which men on motorcycles threw acid on the faces of women they considered improperly dressed. There were also cases of men throwing acid on women who refused their overtures to date or marry them.

In the case of rape, four male witnesses, or three men and two women, are required to convict someone. If convicted, the penalties can be severe, including the death penalty. But women are generally afraid to report rape for fear that they are the ones who will be punished, not the rapists.

Iran does have shelters for women fleeing abuse, run by both state and private organizations, but there are not enough shelters and they do not provide long-term support—the jobs and housing women need to escape abusive situations.

Another form of violence against women is "honor killing," a murder committed or ordered by a husband, father, or other relatives as punishment for damaging the family's reputation. Honor killings are uncommon in cities and most common among nomads, uneducated people, and conservative ethnic minorities living near Iran's borders. The victims are mostly married women suspected of adultery or young girls suspected of having sexual relations with boys. The deaths are often made to look like suicides by self-immolation, and the perpetrators usually get away with short prison sentences or none at all.

The state is also guilty of violence against women. Premarital sex, while extremely common, is technically a crime that can result in a penalty of up to 100 lashes and between 10 days and two months in prison. These penalties are usually reserved for prostitutes.

WHAT ARE THE PROSPECTS FOR CHANGE?

Despite government repression, Iran has an active women's rights movement. Iranian women activists fall into two categories:

Muslim feminists who want to improve women's status by reinterpreting Islamic law in a more gender-equitable way, and secular feminists who try to challenge the power of religion. While these groups have clashed over the years, they have also been able to come together despite their differences to fight for common goals.

Sometimes, Iran's feminists have support from the country's leadership. This was the case during the time of reformist President Khatami from 1997–2005, but his pro-women policies were constantly challenged by conservative institutions like the Guardian Council, which reviews all laws for their adherence to Islamic principles.

The best-known women's rights movement in recent years was the 2006 One Million Signatures Campaign, which called for equal rights in marriage and inheritance, an end to polygamy, and stricter forms of punishment for honor killings and other forms of violence against women. Over 1,000 people from 20 provinces took part in the campaign's training courses. They reached out to the public by collecting signatures from both men and women on the streets and in public places.

Despite the totally peaceful and mild nature of the campaign, the government cracked down on the organizers. It prevented women from holding meetings. People collecting signatures were attacked and arrested. Campaign leaders were imprisoned for "threatening national security." While the group failed to collect one million signatures due to the repression against the organizers, the women did bring the issues of discrimination into the public sphere and contributed to some legal changes, including limiting a husband's right to prevent his wife from taking a job, creating a new marriage contract that gives women the right to divorce, and changing the inheritance law (traditionally a man was entitled to twice as much inheritance as a woman).

In 2016, the government cracked down on women's organizations that were promoting female candidates for the upcoming elections. Over a dozen activists based in Tehran were interrogated by Revolutionary Guards and threatened with imprisonment on the basis of national security.[131]

Despite the risks, women still organize. In May 2017, 180 prominent female journalists, intellectuals, and activists issued a public statement calling for greater female participation in economic life (doubling women's employment), repeal of discriminatory laws, more female sports, and a quota reserving at least 30 percent of cabinet positions for women.[132]

The struggle of Iranian women for equality and a more free society continues.

CHAPTER 7: THE IRANIAN ECONOMY AFTER DECADES OF SANCTIONS

Iran's economy is dependent on oil, but not to the extent of its oil-rich neighbors. It has a well-developed industrial sector and an agricultural sector that produces much of the food the nation consumes. A visitor to Iran will see fantastic bazaars and stores brimming with products both local and imported, with customers haggling over prices. But beneath the veneer of a bustling economy is a system wracked by decades of international sanctions, corruption, and mismanagement.

Even so, Iran is still the second largest economy in the Middle East, after Saudi Arabia. Its population of almost 80 million makes it the most populous nation the Middle East after Egypt, providing an enormous market. With its wealth of natural resources and educated population, even Goldman Sachs has asserted that Iran has the potential to become one of the world's largest economies.[133]

WHAT WAS THE ECONOMY LIKE UNDER THE YEARS OF THE MONARCHY?

The Pahlavi monarchy that ruled Iran from 1925 to 1979 transformed Iran from an agrarian nation into a booming industrial one that included both manufacturing and oil production. It also brought vast inequalities in wealth, corruption, a stark urban/rural divide, and Western corporate involvement that provoked social unrest.

Modern industrial plants jumped from a mere 20 in 1925 to over 800 by 1940. From the 1950s to the 1970s, increased revenue from oil allowed the regime to further expand industrial sectors and state institutions. But the modernization and focus on industry also led the monarchy to create monopolies and alienate the Iranian labor force that had been previously based in agriculture.

One of the issues that most infuriated the people was the fortunes of the royal family, gained through corruption, bribes, extortion from other businesses, and stealing from the national coffers. During the 53 years of the Pahlavi dynasty, the imperial family amassed billions of dollars. One Iranian economist estimated the assets of the entire royal family—which included 63 princes and princesses—at over $20 billion, a staggering sum in 1979.[134] Most of the wealth came from oil revenues from the National Iranian Oil Company, which the family siphoned off into their own Swiss bank accounts. The Pahlavi Foundation was supposedly a charity, but in reality it was an investment house representing the family's business interests. The foundation owned banks, hotels, casinos, construction firms, and trading companies. Members of the royal family, including the Shah's twin sister Princess Ashraf, were alleged to be deeply involved in the drug trade, exporting opium and hashish and importing heroin and cocaine.[135]

On the eve of the revolution, the economic division was stark. While the royal family traveled the European capitals in the lap of luxury, millions of displaced peasants had streamed into the cities, where they lived in decrepit shantytowns without basic services such as running water, electricity, garbage collection, health care, and education.[136] As these types of encampments increased, the government's solution was to declare them illegal and send bulldozers to destroy people's meager homes. Outside major cities like Tehran, conditions were even worse.

Literacy rose, but with 68 percent of adults illiterate and 60 percent of children not finishing primary school, Iran lagged behind other countries in the region. Iranian healthcare languished even farther behind its neighbors, with some of the highest infant mortality and lowest doctor-patient rates in the Middle East.

Instead of addressing the housing shortages, poverty, and the gross socioeconomic inequality, the Pahlavi monarchy spent the majority of the country's budget on themselves, the military, and accommodating Iran's wealthy residents.

WHAT WERE THE ECONOMIC POSITIONS OF THE REVOLUTION?

Equity and social justice were among the proclaimed objectives of the revolution. The lofty goals were part of a quest for an Islamic utopia, where the state would eradicate the elite and establish the rule of the *mostazafan* (oppressed). The state was supposed to be the arbiter and guarantor that would lead to the end of deprivation and poverty.

The revolution was openly antagonistic toward big business and capitalists, especially those affiliated with foreign companies. This led to a major shift in ownership. Banks, insurance companies, and many manufacturing industries were nationalized. Large contracts for nuclear power plants, armaments, and military cooperation were cancelled.

In the early years, takeovers and expropriations of capitalist enterprises were widespread. Revolutionary Islamic Courts confiscated the assets of those found by the Islamic judges to be corrupt. Many businessmen fled the country or shuttered their businesses, and newly formed workers' councils took them over.

Iran's revolutionaries also wanted to disengage from foreign control and from the grip of meddling international institutions, such as the International Monetary Fund (IMF) and the World Bank.

Added to this revolutionary upheaval was the impact of sanctions. In response to the 1979 hostage crisis, the U.S. government froze $12 billion of Iranian government assets in the United States and U.S. banks overseas.

That's not all. A glut in the international oil market from 1985 to 1988 severely depressed prices. The oil boom of the 1970s had been adding over $20 billion a year to Iran's economy; by 1986 oil revenues sunk to less than six billion dollars.

With all these shocks, the economy was in freefall. The gross national product between 1979 and 1981 fell by 64 percent; private investment plummeted by 66 percent.[137]

Plagued by chaotic state-run policies, international sanctions, the enormous financial cost of the war with Iraq, and depressed oil prices, by the end of the Iraq war in 1988 the economic revolutionary project was declared defunct. The search for the Islamic utopia and the claim of establishing rule of the oppressed quietly faded. The Islamic Republic shifted from a populist-revolutionary state to a capitalist one, albeit a capitalist state with a strong state sector.

HOW HAS THE POPULATION FARED?

In the early years, the revolution improved the standard of living and quality of life for many of the nation's poor. Perhaps the greatest achievement was the expansion of educational opportunities, especially for rural families and for women, with increased access to free education from primary school to university. By 1998, the percentage of children in school rose from 60 percent to 90 percent. Another major achievement was improving access to basic services, like electricity, drinking water, and healthcare. One of the best measures of success was the plunge in infant mortality by 1988, dropping from 104 deaths to 25 per 1,000 births.

From the time of the revolution until the end of 2016, life expectancy jumped from 54 years to 75 years; schooling jumped from 9 years to 15 years.[138] But unemployment and inflation took their toll on the public's well-being. General unemployment in 2017 was over 12 percent, but youth unemployment was a staggering 30 percent. Underemployment was also rife.

The 50 percent plunge in the value of the rial in 2012 wiped out the savings of many middle class families. This dramatic devaluation was due mainly to oil and banking sanctions, but some also blamed it on the free-spending policies of President Ahmadinejad. Elected on the slogan "put the oil money on the *sofreh*" (the mat Iranians sit on to eat), President Ahmadinejad took a populist turn, expanding credit, providing cheap housing loans to the poor, and subsidizing gasoline.

These subsidies saddled the economy with an enormous annual bill of $100 billion. In 2010 the government eliminated the energy subsidies, but began a universal cash transfer program of about $40 per person per month to all Iranians, including children, to compensate for the elimination.

The policies fueled inflation just as sanctions began to have an impact.[139] According to one study, the percentage of Iranian families living in poverty increased during Ahmadinejad's term (from 2005 to 2013) from 22 percent to 40 percent.[140]

With the economic devastation caused by 2011 sanctions, workers have seen the value of their wages plummet. The government raised the minimum wage by 25 percent in 2013, but even official criteria deemed this new wage to be just one-third of a living wage for Tehran. A 2016 report by the Iranian parliament said the minimum monthly wage for workers was about $214, while the national poverty line was about $600 a month.

These economic hardships sparked the protests that spread throughout the country at the end of December 2017.

WHO CONTROLS THE NATION'S MAIN RESOURCES?

Iran has a vibrant agricultural sector, employing about 18 percent of workers, while some 34 percent of workers are employed in factories. Many of the rest—nearly one-third of the employed workforce—are self-employed in traditional occupations such as rug makers, carpenters, taxi and truck drivers, street vendors, and shopkeepers.

But most of Iran's economy—by some estimates as much as 60 percent—is in the hands of the state. While it is dominated by oil and gas, the state sector also includes all large-scale industry, foreign trade, major minerals, banking insurance, power generation, radio and television, telephone serves, aviation, shipping, and railroads. There is a significant cooperative sector that operates in accordance with sharia law.

The state sector also manufactures most of its own weapons, from aircraft to artillery to drones—some of which are reverse-engineered from captured U.S. models.

Out of necessity, the role of the private sector has been increasing. A 2003 constitutional amendment allowed 80 percent of state assets to be privatized. Between 2005 and 2010, the government sold half of its $120 billion assets. Many assets, however, were not really privatized since they ended up either in the hands of the Islamic Revolutionary Guard Corps, Iran's security force and the most powerful economic actor in the country, or with its affiliated corporations and religious charities.

The IRGC controls an enormous part of the nation's economy—by some estimates up to one third. Through a tangled web of subsidiaries and trusts, the IRGC has ties to over one hundred companies and an annual revenue of over $12 billion. It gets billions of dollars in no-bid contracts from the Ministry of Petroleum and from government infrastructure projects. It also runs the phone company, makes cars, and builds bridges and roads. Some allege that through its control of the border and ports, the IRGC is also involved in smuggling all types of good, including drugs.

Another unique feature of Iran's economy is the role of large, quasi-state, religious foundations, called *bonyads*. *Bonyads* are a consortium of over 120 tax-exempt organizations that get government subsidies and religious donations. They are under the control of the Supreme Leader. According to some estimates, they control over half the state budget and account for somewhere between 20 to 40 percent of the economy. They operate everything from farms to hotels to shipping lines, and are not subject to audits or the nation's accounting laws.

Established shortly after the revolution, the foundations confiscated billions of dollars in assets from the former royal family, banks, and elites who fled the country. Most of the foundations are exempt from taxes and are involved in activities ranging from trade and commerce to social services and cultural affairs. They have become some of the biggest economic powerhouses in the Middle East. Most of them are the individual fiefs of powerful clerics, and their size crowds out smaller private competitors who might be more efficient.

Seen as unfair competition with the other private businesses, these companies have a reputation of being corrupt, overstaffed, and only viable because of government support.

ARE TRADE UNIONS ALLOWED?

Iran's labor movement has a long history of defending workers' rights. Oil workers played a key role in overthrowing the Shah. After the revolution, a worker-friendly labor law was passed that guaranteed a 40-hour week and made it hard to lay off workers without proof of a serious offense. Employing personnel on consecutive six-month contracts to avoid paying benefits was deemed illegal.

But with the Iran-Iraq war, workers suffered. Conscripted, many young men fought and died on the front lines. Employment also plummeted, since much of the nation's infrastructure was destroyed, especially in the southwestern part of the country. The economic chaos of the early years also led to a crackdown on workers. Independent unions were destroyed, and labor disputes began to be settled by state-sponsored Islamic Labor Councils, which must be approved by employers and usually rule in favor of the employers.[141]

In 1997, temporary contracts were made legal, leading to the massive erosion of permanent positions. In 2002, businesses with under ten employees were deemed exempt from the labor law, further eroding workers' conditions. Employers try to keep their employees under ten so they can hire workers without contracts.

Iran is a member of the International Labor Organization (ILO), which calls for independent trade unions, but the unions that do exist are closely monitored by the state, including the official state union called the Workers' House. Strikes and work stoppages, mostly by transport, education, and factory workers, are common but illegal and often suppressed, including through the imprisonment of labor leaders.

During the reform era of President Khatami, there was a new wave of trade unionism, including by petrochemical workers, construction workers, sugarcane workers, teachers, and bus drivers, but even these were suppressed. In 2004, construction workers at a copper plant operated by a Chinese contractor held a strike calling on the company to fulfill its hiring promises. Security forces attacked the strikers, leaving four workers killed, 300 wounded, and many arrested.[142]

In 2005, workers at the Tehran Bus Company formed an independent union called the Vahed Bus Workers Union. A strike in 2005 led to the imprisonment of hundreds of bus drivers and their supporters. Soon after, a national teachers association (ITTA) was created, organizing strikes against low wages, and many other sectors began independent unions. But when President Ahmadinejad came to power in 2005, most of these union leaders were arrested. ITTA leader Esmail Abdi was sentenced to six years in prison for "distributing propaganda against the establishment" and "disrupting public order and security."

With the signing of the Iran nuclear deal and lifting of some sanctions, labor leaders perceived a new opportunity to organize. "Iran is very eager to attract European companies and do business with them, and this could be a chance for Iranian activists, since all EU companies are committed to guaranteeing responsible business behavior," said Hadi Ghaemi, executive director of the New York-based Center for Human Rights in Iran.[143]

WHAT IS THE ROLE OF OIL AND GAS?

Iran has about 10 percent of the world's proven oil reserves and 15 percent of its gas reserves. According to the U.S. Energy Information Administration, Iran has the world's second-largest natural gas reserves and the fourth-largest oil reserves. Oil exports contribute about 80 percent of the nation's public revenue.

The history of oil in Iran dates back to 1901, when British speculator William D'Arcy received a concession from the Iranian government giving him exclusive rights to prospect for oil. After searching for years without success in finding sellable amounts of oil, D'Arcy and team were about to go bankrupt when in 1908, a fifty-foot gusher of petroleum shot up the drilling rig, revealing such large quantities of oil that a new corporate structure was created to work the concession.[144] This led to the formation of the Anglo-Persian Oil Company and direct British control over Iranian oil fields.

In 1950, Iran attempted to nationalize the industry and created the National Iranian Oil Company, but three years later, U.S. and British intelligence agencies overthrew the Iranian prime minister committed to nationalization and reasserted their claim to half of the profits.[145]

The 1979 revolution brought a reversal of fortunes. Iran cut the international deals, and the state-owned NIOC took full control of the country's oil. Driven by the need for revenue during the exhausting Iran-Iraq war, Iran adopted a more aggressive approach to oil to maximize exports, investing billions to expand oil fields and export to Africa, Asia, and Europe.[146]

Despite efforts to diversify, Iran's economy remains dependent on oil and gas. When some international sanctions were lifted in January 2016, Iran was producing 1.5 million barrels of oil per day. Within five months, it had bumped up production to 2.6 million barrels per day, with plans to increase production to 5 million barrels per day by 2021.[147]

While this allowed foreign currency to flow in, it did little to create jobs because the oil sector is not labor-intensive.

WHAT HAVE BEEN THE EFFECTS OF SANCTIONS?

It's a wonder that the Iranian economy functions as well as it does, given the crippling restrictions it is been subjected to since the time of the 1979 revolution. Sanctions started with the U.S. Embassy hostage crisis, when the Carter administration banned Iranian oil imports, froze $12 billion in Iranian government assets in the United States, and imposed an embargo on travel to Iran. Some of these restrictions were lifted when the hostages were released, but the Reagan administration, after the 1983 bombing of a U.S. Marine compound in Lebanon, blocked World Bank loans to Iran and later banned all US imports from Iran.

Starting in 1995, the Clinton administration used sanctions to punish Iran for links to groups it defined as terrorists—Hezbollah, Hamas, and Palestinian Islamic Jihad. The administration placed a total trade and investment embargo on Iran. Congress went even further with a 1996 sanctions bill pressuring foreign companies to refrain from investing in Iran's oil and gas industry. In 2005, the Bush administration froze the assets of individuals and firms, including Russian and Chinese companies, that it deemed involved in Iran's "support for terrorism" and its nuclear and missile programs. It also prosecuted individuals and companies changed with selling weapons to Iran.

The Obama administration continued and intensified these sanctions. Congressional measures passed in 2010 targeted insurance companies that insured Iranian shipping, and squeezed the oil and gas sector further. Sanctions had already cobbled Iran's refineries, forcing this oil-rich nation to import 30 percent of its refined gasoline. New bans targeted non-U.S. firms supplying Iran with refined petroleum products.

Through the U.S. Treasury Department's Office of Foreign Assets Control, billions of dollars in penalties have been inflicted

on U.S. branches of foreign-owned banks for sanctions violations. As a result, many banks adopted a "de-risking" strategy,
refusing to conduct even permissible business with Iran for fear
of coming under regulatory scrutiny. U.S. measures also greatly
restricted the access of Iranian banks to the global financial system, as well as its Central Bank's access to its own $150 billion of
foreign exchange money that the U.S. froze—funds that were only
released after the nuclear deal was signed.

By 2010, other major European countries joined U.S. sanctions
in a concerted effort to force Iran to cease its nuclear program.
These crippling measures included a ban on dealings with Iran's
Central Bank, a ban on imports of Iranian oil, and a ban on trade in
gold, diamonds, and precious metals. In 2012, the European Union
joined the U.S. effort to close off Iran's oil trade. The pressure further increased when Iranian banks were shut out of the SWIFT
global electronic payments system.

A look at the website of the Treasury Department's Office of
Foreign Assets Control shows the vast concoction of bureaucratic
punishments the U.S. government cooked up over the years to
squeeze Iran economically. They include 27 Executive Orders, 11
Statutes, 23 Interpretive Guidance documents.[148] They are meant
to scare U.S. companies from even contemplating deals with Iran,
but they are also meant to influence foreign companies around the
globe.

Many Iranians interpreted these draconian measures not as a
way to force a nuclear deal but as an insidious international plan
to weaken Iran to the benefit of pro-Western governments in the
region, like Israel and Saudi Arabia. President Ahmadinejad called
them "the heaviest economic onslaught on a nation in history.
Every day, all our banking and trade activities and our agreements
are being blocked."[149]

An Iranian women's rights activist reflected, "The sanctions started 32 years ago. I don't know of any people who have suffered these kinds of sanctions over such a long period, except Palestinians and Cubans. They toppled our democratically elected government in 1953. After the revolution, they helped prolong the war with Iraq, and as such helped push the Iranian government to the right. I don't know what the West has gained from all this. I only ask: Why do they hate us so much?"[150]

One of the most difficult issues for businesses has been access to financing, especially for smaller businesses. Thousands of businesses were forced to close, leaving workers stranded. With a constrained economy and lack of investment, many educated Iranians left to seek employment abroad, leading to a brain drain among some of the nation's brightest young people.

Economic sanctions are blunt policy instruments that often harm the civilian population far more than the state. In the case of Iran, sanctions destroyed the purchasing power of ordinary citizens. Prices for food, rent, fuel, and other basic necessities rose steeply— by 100 percent in some instances. Despite subsidies intended to help the poor, in 2012 prices for staples such as milk, bread, yogurt, and vegetables doubled, prompting food riots. Middle class families began living on rice and beans. Many medicines for serious illnesses became scarce or prohibitively expensive. Theft, something rare in Iran, shot up. Imported goods became unaffordable, and the government was forced to embark on an emergency campaign to substitute imports with domestic production.

Sanctions have also led to greater corruption. In 2016, Transparency International ranked Iran among the world's more corrupt countries, with a rating of 131 out of 176 nations.[151] Often the only way to get basic goods is through the black market, so government entities and businesses that control the black market reap windfall profits. Paying bribes to get access to scarce goods or to reduce taxes, fees, and custom duties became routine. And the hardline Islamic Revolutionary Guards Corps, with its unfair advantages over private businesses, gained control over vast sectors of the country's economy. This also means that, while one of the goals of sanctions is to weaken the government, sanctions actually strengthen the government's hand vis-a-vis the public. People become more dependent on the government for their economic survival.

Sanctions and corruption have also led to a yawning wealth gap between the rich and the poor that mirrors the pre-revolutionary society of haves and have-nots. When Mahmoud Ahmadinejad was president, he complained that 60 percent of the nation's wealth was controlled by just 300 people. Luxury apartments and fancy cars line the streets in the wealthy neighborhoods in North Tehran while families cram together in small, rented rooms in the poorer South Tehran. In the rural areas, especially areas depleted from drought, the poverty is even worse,

Another insidious, little-known effect of sanctions has been the environmental impact. Not only was Iran barred from selling its crude oil, but it was also barred from importing refined gasoline. This forced the country to quickly come up with a way to refine its own oil. The result was poor-quality oil, leading to tremendous air pollution in the cities and skyrocketing deaths from respiratory diseases. In Tehran, the days of "healthy air" dropped from 300 days in 2009 to 150 days in 2011.[152] Air quality got so bad that there were days the capital city had to be shut down for people's safety and health. As one reporter quipped, "No longer are Iranians merely suffering from the economic effects of wide-ranging international sanctions; they are literally choking to death from them."[153]

There is one silver lining from these decades of economic strangulation: a focus on self-reliance. Cut off from the outside, the government's call for a "resistance economy" has promoted decades of local development and diversification. Iranian researchers and entrepreneurs have stepped in to fill the thousands of voids, showing the remarkable creativity and skill of the Iranian people. It has also helped preserve Iranian culture. Without a Starbucks on every corner, local tea shops thrive; without U.S. fast food chains, Iranians continue to appreciate their delicious Persian cuisine. There are pseudo-American chains like Pizza Hat and Kabooki Fried Chicken, but the restaurants are locally owned and operated.

DID SANCTIONS BRING IRAN TO THE NEGOTIATING TABLE?

The short answer is "not really."

The common assumption in the U.S. is that the pressure of sanctions forced a crippled Iran to cry uncle and make a deal. President Obama offered up this narrative, as did his staff—and even detractors of the diplomatic initiatives.[154] The reality, however, is more complex.

What most of the argument ignores is that the Iranians played their own pressure track as well. In what could be described as a game of diplomatic chicken, the Iranians met pressure with pressure by accelerating their nuclear program.[155] From 2009, when Obama's first attempt at a negotiated settlement failed, to 2013, when talks finally bore fruit, the number of Iranian centrifuges and the amount of enriched uranium increased dramatically. The nation's technological know-how became so advanced that they were less than three months away from having enough fissile material for a bomb.[156]

So the fact that the Iranians had accelerated their program in response to the sanctions would suggest that the sanctions achieved the opposite of their intended objective.

Several other points also bear noting. First, implying that sanctions brought Iran to the table ignores the fact that Iran was already at the table. Negotiations had been ongoing since 2009, albeit in fits and starts and with little to no progress. Nonetheless, Iran had already committed to talks. The team around President Rouhani, particularly Foreign Minister Javad Zarif, had displayed a willingness to engage diplomatically. Zarif was already engaged with the United States in another diplomatic initiative, helping to bring together the various factions within Afghanistan for the signing of the Bonn Agreement.

The problem was not Iran's willingness to negotiate, but the terms of the negotiations. It was only after Obama recognized Iran's right to enrich that progress was made. After years of frustrations and talking over each other with regurgitated demands, Obama finally relented. But so did the Iranians. They allowed for a robust and invasive inspections regime led by the International Atomic Energy Agency, and they agreed to limits on enrichment. Thus, compromise was the final push needed to get an agreement.

In the end, no single element made the deal a success. This isn't to deny that sanctions hurt the Iranians, they did. But they weren't the decisive factor bringing the Iran to the table or creating the conditions for the agreement signed on July 14, 2015 between the six countries involved in the talks.

WHAT HAPPENED AFTER THE SIGNING OF THE NUCLEAR DEAL?

Some $100 billion in frozen assets were released after the completion of the nuclear deal, which went mostly to pay outstanding debts and modernize the oil industry and the air fleet. Other sanctions, however, remained. Those were sanctions imposed in response to Iran's missile program and sanctions in opposition to Iran's ties with groups like Hamas and Hezbollah. So while Iran did reap some benefit from the lifting of nuclear-related sanctions, it was not as much as expected. Many Iranians felt cheated by the deal, as their lives failed to improve. In a January 2017 poll, 73 percent of Iranians said the nuclear deal had not improved their living conditions.[157]

At the end of December 2017, the economic dissatisfaction erupted in protests that roiled the country for several weeks. The demonstrators voiced their discontent over cuts in government subsidies, economic mismanagement, corruption, and wealth inequality. While the government managed to crush the uprising, it felt the heat and new economic reforms may well be in the offing.

The government is hoping that economic relief might come with the inking of several major deals with foreign companies anxious to get a foothold in such a potentially enormous market. One such deal is with the American company Boeing and its European competitor Airbus, a deal to sell up to 140 commercial planes. The Iranian government is desperate to upgrade its aging civilian fleet. The wear and tear from operating the same planes for decades, and the inability to buy spare parts, has led to plane crashes and the deaths of hundreds of passengers. But President Trump might scuttle the deal, a deal that Boeing says would support up to 118,000 American jobs.

Another major investment involves the French energy giant Total. In July 2017, Total announced its plan to invest $1 billion in Iran to develop the giant South Pars gas field, the largest natural gas field in the world. This was the biggest deal by a Western energy company in Iran in more than a decade. Royal Dutch Shell also signed several memorandums of understanding for projects in Iran.

The French carmaker PSA had been heavily invested in Iran since the 1960s. At that time it claimed almost 30 percent of Iran's car market. Under the weight of international sanctions, it was forced to pull out in 2011. With the easing of restrictions in 2016, it re-entered the market, committing $320 million to manufacture Citroen cars in Iran. In the meantime, however, Chinese rivals had grabbed up a good chunk of the car market.[158]

India has been one of Iran's most reliable trading partners. In 2017, a consortium of Indian businesses announced it would offer up to $11 billion to develop another of Iran's natural gas fields. Iran is the second-largest supplier of crude oil to India, and India is one of the largest foreign investors in Iran's oil and gas industry. However, international restrictions have impacted these investments as well. With U.S. banking restrictions still in place in 2018, India could not trade with Iran in dollars and had to revert to payments in rupees or euros.

WHAT ABOUT IRAN'S ECONOMIC RELATIONSHIP WITH CHINA?

During a decade of international restrictions, Western companies dealing in everything from oil to communications to cars had been replaced by Chinese ones. China became Iran's number one investor and trade partner. Iranian streets soon overflowed with Chinese consumer products.

For Iranian leaders, China represents an important outlet for international trade and finance. For China, Iran is a vital transport and logistics hub. China is providing $1.8 billion to establish a high-speed rail connection linking key Iranian cities of Tehran, Qom, and Isfahan, and another $1.5 billion to electrify the rail line from Tehran to the city of Mashad. In exchange, Iran is slashing transit tariffs for Chinese goods. The Iranian route from Tehran to the east will be part of China's 3,200 kilometer New Silk Road rail link that starts in China's western Xinjiang province and ends in the Iranian capital, connecting Kazakhstan, Kyrgyzstan, Uzbekistan, and Turkmenistan along the way.

China also became a key source of weapons and nuclear technology. But the Chinese, too, have been subjected to U.S. pressure, and Iranians have complained of Chinese failures to deliver on promised deals. Iranian producers also complained that cheap Chinese imports undercut local manufacturing. Iranian leaders have also been wary of relying too much on China and have been trying to work with a greater spectrum of foreign companies.

*****

Despite these major deals, foreign investment has fallen short of anticipated levels. The uncertainly about sanctions and the nuclear deal made international banks reluctant to finance projects and companies jittery abut the risks posed by investing in Iran.

The Trump administration and the U.S. Congress continue to destabilize Iran's economy. Instead of lifting restrictions, they impose new ones. The Trump administration argues that strengthening the Iranian economy by lifting sanctions just shores up the regime and its support for groups such as Hezbollah and Hamas. But European nations and human rights advocates argue that supporting Iran's economy is the best way to boost political moderates. They also argue that integrating Iran into the global economy creates incentives for the country to abide by the nuclear agreement and to reduce tensions in the region.

A similar debate has been occurring inside Iran. Political and religious hardliners have opposed opening up the nation's economy to foreign capital, especially to Western businesses. These conservatives have reaped the benefits of controlling the nation's key industries and have much to lose from a more open economy.

On the other side is President Rouhani and his supporters, who want more international investment, especially from the West. Most Iranians support the opening as well, but not if the benefits remain in the pockets of the elites.

In any case, the government is under intense internal pressure to improve the economy and spread the gains. The very future of the regime rests on its ability to deliver more economic benefits to the working class and the urban middle class, and to create more job oppportunities for the nation's restless youth.

CHAPTER 8: IRAN'S RELATIONS WITH THE US AND THE WEST

Iran has a long history of interacting with the rest of the world—initially as the various empires discussed in earlier chapters, and now as the Islamic Republic. The resentment and suspicion of foreign interference found in the Iranian political culture are a direct result of historic deals with foreigners that took power away from the local elites, including *bazaaris* and the *clerics*.

Through the 1800s to the early half of the 1900s, Russia and Britain were the main foreign interventionist forces and therefore became the focus of the public's vitriol. As the 20th century evolved, the United States began playing a larger role in Iran, due primarily to Cold War dynamics. As American policy in Iran came to resemble the earlier Russian and British imperial policies, anger towards the United States grew. That resentment boiled over and was a key factor in the 1979 revolution.

HOW AND WHEN DID THE U.S. BECOME THE FOCAL POINT FOR IRAN'S INTERACTIONS WITH THE WEST?

Starting in the 1830s, American missionaries began arriving in Iran, but it would take another 20 years before there would be any official diplomatic recognition between the two nations. That came in 1856 with the signing of a Treaty of Commerce and Navigation. Even then, the U.S. role remained minimal.

Iran really became important to the United States after World War II, in the context of the burgeoning Cold War with the Soviets. During World War II, the Allies had agreed to leave Iran six months after the war ended. Yet after victory was finally sealed in September 1945, U.S. and British forces left Iran within the agreed timeframe, but Soviet forces remained, expanding their areas of control and supporting local Kurdish and Azeri separatists.

The Shah secured U.S. support to push the Soviets out by painting the crisis in Cold War colors. U.S. diplomatic pressure and Iranian negotiations were successful in demanding a Soviet withdrawal. In 1947, Iran was included in the Truman Doctrine, the policy established by President Truman that said the United States would use its economic, political, and military power to contain Soviet threats anywhere in the world. As Iran became increasingly critical to blocking Soviet expansion, American support for Iran's monarchy increased.

The U.S. alliance with Iran came crashing down in 1953, however, when the recently inaugurated American President Dwight D. Eisenhower approved CIA plans to overthrow the government of elected Prime Minister Mohammad Mossadegh, who had incurred the wrath of both British and American oil companies and governments by nationalized oil fields. Once Mossadegh was deposed, the U.S. became the main ally of the new Shah and helped to develop the Iranian military and infamous secret police.

For many Iranians, this was the moment that the U.S. went from friend to foe. Originally thought to be a supporter of Iran's movement towards democracy, the U.S. had instead orchestrated a coup. This resentment would be one of the major driving forces, 25 years later, when a popular protest movement ultimately overthrew the U.S.-backed Shah. It also lies at the very foundation of the current government's anti-Americanism.

As the CIA's first successful covert operation to overthrow a government that refused to bend to U.S. economic and political interests, the overthrow of Mossadegh also became a model for similar operations around the globe, such as the overthrow of Guatemalan President Arbenz in 1954, Congolese Prime Minister Patrice Lumuba in 1960, and the failed intervention in Cuba in 1961.

HOW DID THE REVOLUTION AFFECT THE U.S. RELATIONSHIP?

America's role in ousting Mossadegh vaulted it to the top of Iran's most-hated list, a position once held by the Russians and the British. The United States became the focus for the anti-imperialists within Iran.

Tensions ran high in 1963 when the U.S. and Iran signed a Status of Forces Agreement (SOFA) that gave Americans immunity from punishment under the law. This meant that all American personnel accused of wrongdoing in Iran, including the large number of U.S. military personnel who were training the Shah's military forces, would be free from prosecution by Iranian authorities.

A relatively minor cleric at the time, Ayatollah Ruhollah Khomeini, used this agreement to speak out against the Shah and the United States. He gave a famous speech decrying that in the eyes of the Shah and his American allies, Iranians were worth less than American dogs.[159] The Shah responded by forcing Khomeini into exile in 1964.

Over the years, anti-Shah and anti-U.S. tensions continued to mount. Both the U.S. State Department and intelligence services missed the writing on the wall, underestimating the breadth and depth of the opposition. In one evaluation, six months prior to the 1979 revolution, the CIA reported that "Iran is not in a revolutionary or even pre-revolutionary situation."[160]

U.S. President Jimmy Carter seemed oblivious to the changing landscape. After pressuring the Shah to improve his human rights record, President Carter visited Iran in late December 1977. During a New Year's toast, Carter described Iran as "an island of stability in one of the most troublesome regions in the world."[161] In the same speech, he talked about how popular the Shah was among Iranians. In a little over a year, the Shah was ousted from power.

Shortly after the Shah fled, Ayatollah Khomeini, who had been the main face of the growing opposition movement, returned from exile in France. Despite Khomeini's anti-American rhetoric, some U.S. officials felt it was necessary to meet with the new revolutionary government. As 1979 progressed, however, anti-American sentiment grew, especially when President Carter allowed the Shah to enter the U.S. as a "private citizen" to receive cancer treatment. The Shah's presence in the United States was seen by many Iranians as a disgrace and an insult that ignored the enormous pain and suffering they had endured under his rule, with the approval of the U.S. government.

For Iran's revolutionaries, many of whom blamed the US for the 1953 coup, Carter's decision was a clear signal that the Shah was planning a counter-revolution with America's help.[162] They wanted the Shah extradited, tried, and executed for his crimes against the Iranian population. The revolutionaries did not get their wish, but they did find a new target—the U.S. Embassy.

HOW AND WHY DID THE TAKEOVER OF THE U.S. EMBASSY HAPPEN?

Originally planned as a sit in, on November 4, 1979, students climbed the fences and stormed the U.S. Embassy compound. Ransacking offices and detaining embassy personnel, their radical actions surprised both the U.S. government and Iran's provisional government. Khomeini originally backed a plan to forcibly remove the protesters from the embassy, but then endorsed their actions once he realized he could use the seizure to solidify power. The revolution had risked spiraling out of control as the various factions were openly clashing in the streets. The embassy seizure was a symbolic way to synergize around a cause while also showing that Iran could stand up for itself. The provisional government resigned due to its disapproval of the takeover.

Fifty-two American diplomats were held hostage for 444 days. This act marked a breaking point in relations between Iran and the United States. Diplomatic relations were severed and have officially been frozen ever since. Americans saw the takeover as a breach of the one inviolable law governing relations between countries—the sanctity of embassies. The revolutionaries viewed it as a way to prevent a counter-coup and to hit back at decades of foreign interference in Iran's internal affairs.

Attempts at negotiating for the release of the hostages were stymied by Ayatollah Khomeini's prohibition on speaking to American officials and a lack of overall stability within Iran. With Khomeini's goals of crushing other factions and solidifying power, settling with the U.S. was not in the cards. If he had negotiated, he would have gone against his own narrative. Meanwhile, the U.S. could not adopt a policy of patience, since Carter was in the middle of a re-election campaign. And what country is patient when their diplomats are being held hostage?

As the domestic pressure on President Carter mounted, in April 1980 he approved an ill-fated rescue attempt called Operation Eagle Claw. It failed in large part because a severe desert sandstorm caused several helicopters to collide as they were taking off for Tehran. Eight American servicemen were killed, and the operation was aborted.

Just a few months later, the Shah, Mohammad Reza Pahlavi, died of cancer. Khomeini responded by tasking his subordinates with finding a solution to the hostage crisis.

In the middle of negotiations to release the hostages, Iraq invaded Iran, delaying talks until November 1980. By the time an agreement was signed, Carter had already lost the presidential election to Ronald Reagan. In a slap in the face to President Carter, Khomeini delayed the release of the hostages until the day Ronald Reagan was sworn into office.

For many older Americans, the lens through which they view Iran is still tinted by the hostage crisis. Each night, from the very beginning of the crisis, the U.S. press updated the public on the status of the hostages and efforts to get them released. Every night for 444 days, Ted Koppel's ABC News special *America Held Hostage: The Iran Crisis* (which later became *Nightline*) reminded Americans that Iranians had kidnapped their diplomats. But for many Iranians, the U.S. history of violating their sovereignty outweighs their responsibility for the hostage crisis.

WHAT POSITION DID THE U.S. TAKE DURING THE 1980–88 IRAN-IRAQ WAR?

Officially, the United States remained neutral during the war that broke out in 1980 after Iraq invaded Iran, but, in reality, it was arming both sides. Shortly after taking office in 1981, the Reagan administration secretly worked with Israel to ship several billion dollars of American weapons to Iran, despite the U.S. embargo against such sales. Then in 1982, when the CIA warned Reagan that Iraq was on the verge of being beaten on the battlefield by Iran, the U.S. government secretly provided Iraq with highly classified intelligence, including on Iranian troop movements, and covertly shipped American weapons to Iraq.[163] Basically, the United States was arming both sides so that neither side would dominate this key oil region. By 1983, however, the U.S. began to favor Iraq, turning a blind eye while U.S. arms dealers sold sophisticated Soviet arms to Iraqi strongman Saddam Hussein.

Even worse, the Reagan administration sold Iraq biological agents, including anthrax, and vital ingredients for chemical weapons—all the while knowing that the Iraqi leader Saddam Hussein was regularly using these horrific weapons against the Iranian people and against his own Iraqi citizens. The 1983 photo of Middle East envoy Donald Rumsfeld shaking hands with Saddam Hussein is chilling. Years later, in 2003, the U.S. government used the very biological weapons it sold Hussein as a pretext to invade Iraq. A morbid joke at that time had George W. Bush saying, "We know Saddam Hussein has chemical weapons—we have the receipts."

WHY DID THE U.S. SHOOT DOWN AN IRANIAN AIRBUS IN 1988?

During the brutal eight years of the Iran-Iraq war, Iraq and then Iran used air attacks to target foreign tankers transporting each other's oil exports through the Persian Gulf. This led the U.S. and other nations to deploy warships to protect their tankers in international waters.

On July 3, 1988, a terrible tragedy occurred: U.S. personnel on the warship *USS Vincennes* shot down a commercial passenger airline, Iran Air Flight 655, which was flying along its official route from Tehran to Dubai. All 290 people on board—274 passengers and 16 crew—were killed.

According to the U.S. government, this was a regrettable accident. The crew incorrectly identified the Iranian Airbus A300 as an attacking F-14 Tomcat fighter.

Most Iranians, however, believed it was a deliberate war crime. This belief was reinforced when the U.S. government tried to mislead the world about the details of the incident. It made a series of false claims that the plane was not on a normal flight path but was diving toward the ship rather than climbing after taking off from Bandar Abbas airport in southern Iran; that its identification transponder was not working or had been altered; and that the *Vincennes* was either rushing to the aid of a merchant ship or pursuing hostile Iranian patrol boats.

Months before the plane was shot down, air traffic controllers and the crews of other warships in the Persian Gulf had been warning that poorly trained U.S. crews, especially the gung-ho captain and crew of the *Vincennes* (or "Robocruiser," as other crews had nicknamed it), were constantly misidentifying civilian aircrafts over the Persian Gulf, making this horrific massacre entirely predictable.

Adding insult to injury when, two years later, the U.S. Navy awarded combat medals to the warship's captain and crew. The town of Vincennes, Indiana, for which the ship was named, even launched a fundraising campaign for a monument. The monument was not to remember the tragedy or the Iranians killed, but to honor the ship and its crew.

In 1996, in response to an Iranian lawsuit at the International Court of Justice, the U.S. agreed to a settlement, granting $213,000 per passenger to the victim's families. But the U.S. government still refused to formally apologize or acknowledge wrongdoing.

While most Americans have no memory of this incident, in Iran the date of the deaths of 290 Iranian citizens at the hands of the U.S. military is marked every year just as the 9/11 attack is remembered every year in the United States. To some Iranians, it is just one more example of the callousness of U.S. policy.

WAS IRAN INVOLVED IN 1983 MARINE BOMBING?

Another incident that has impacted U.S.-Iranian relations was the bombing in 1983 of the U.S. Marine barracks in Beirut, Lebanon that killed 241 U.S. service personnel. The explosion came from a truck bomb at the compound. There were 1,800 Marines stationed in Beirut at the time as part of a multinational peacekeeping force. The bombing was traced to the Iranian-affiliated militia group, Hezbollah, and the U.S. accused Iran of being behind the attack. In April 2016, the U.S. Supreme Court ruled that frozen Iranian bank assets could be used to pay $1.75 billion to the survivors and family members of those killed. As of early 2018, however, those funds have still not been disbursed to the families.

WHAT WAS THE IRAN-CONTRA AFFAIR? HOW DID THAT AFFECT THE RELATIONSHIP?

Even though the U.S. and Iran did not have official relations after 1979, there were still points of engagement. In most cases, these have been one-off affairs and limited in scope.

One of the earliest such cases was the issue known as the Iran-Contra Affair. Starting in 1985, only a few years after the U.S. Embassy hostages were released and ties officially severed, Iran, the U.S., and Israel found themselves entangled in an illegal, secret web of confusion, misaligned interests, and shady middlemen.

Enmeshed in a brutal war with Iraq, Iran was in dire need of spare parts for its military, but there was a U.S. embargo on selling arms to Iran. At the same time, the Reagan administration was anxious to bring home seven Americans being held hostage in Lebanon by Hezbollah, a paramilitary group with ties to Iran. Despite the American position that it would never negotiate with hostage takers, the Reagan administration decided to sell weapons to Iran in exchange for Iran's help in freeing the U.S. hostages.

Given the illegality of selling weapons to Iran, however, the Israelis were brought in as go-betweens. Their job was to ship weapons to Iran, and then the U.S. would resupply Israel.

This scheme became even more complicated when U.S. Marine Lt. Colonel Oliver North of the National Security Council became involved in late 1985. He modified the plan so that a portion of the proceeds from the weapon sales to Iran would be diverted to fund the "Contras," an armed rebel group in Nicaragua that was trying to overthrow the leftist Sandinistas. There was a congressional prohibition on arming the Contras, so this was an attempt to subvert the prohibition.

This sordid affair now involved violating one congressional order against arms sales to Iran, then using the proceeds from that illegal operation to fund a project violating another congressional order banning the provision of arms to the Contras. Both acts breached the constitution.

The scheme was doomed from the start. When the first weapons shipment arrived in Iran, only one of the seven American hostages in Lebanon was released. The Iranians realized that it was in their best interest to slow walk their obligations so they could maintain the flow of weapons and spare parts. With two subsequent shipments, two more hostages were released, but two more hostages were taken. The U.S., for its part, sent old weapons and never agreed to send enough to alter the outcome of the Iran-Iraq war. Both sides were playing each other and had arrived at an impasse.

U.S. officials covertly traveled to Iran to work out a new deal but were blindsided when reports of the meeting were leaked to the media and made worldwide headlines.[164] "Arms for Hostages" did not make good PR for either side, and all negotiations ceased.

America's PR nightmare became even worse when it was revealed that proceeds from the weapons sales were used to purchase arms for the Nicaraguan Contras in flagrant violation of U.S. law.[165] Fourteen of Reagan's aides were indicted, including the Secretary of Defense and two national security advisors, and 11 were convicted. Reagan's presidency was tarnished by the sordid affair, and it was a further setback for U.S.-Iranian relations. None of the 14 went to jail, and President George H.W. Bush, who was vice president under Reagan, pardoned all of them in his final days in office.

WHAT SHIFTS TOOK PLACE IN THE 1990S?

In the waning days of the 1980s, Iran and Iraq agreed to a ceasefire, and Ayatollah Khomeini passed away. There was hope that the subsequent increase in trade between Iran and the U.S., coupled with the new Supreme Leader Ayatollah Ali Khamenei, would lead to improved relations. U.S. hostages were still being held in Lebanon, but Iran seemed more amenable to working for their release. Additionally, Saddam Hussein's decision to invade Kuwait in 1990 lent more credibility to Iran's assertion that he was the aggressor during their eight-year war.

When President Reagan's vice president, George H.W. Bush, was elected to succeed him, Bush seemed like a candidate who could help lead the détente. In his inaugural address, he promised to "reciprocate goodwill with goodwill." Iranian President Akbar Hashemi Rafsanjani saw this as a positive sign that the Americans were willing to take concrete steps to improve their relationship. To test their resolve, Rafsanjani pulled the necessary strings to have the Americans held hostage in Lebanon released. But the Bush administration reneged on its offer to meet goodwill with goodwill, damaging the potential for rapprochement.

Cooperation with Iran did occur during the 1991 Gulf War, when the U.S.-led Operation Desert Storm pushed Iraq out of Kuwait. While not directly joining the fight against Iraq, the Iranians allowed coalition airplanes overflight rights. After the war, Iran tried to build a Gulf-based security coalition that could provide regional stability.

The Bush administration, however, had its own plans. It organized a conference to discuss the future of the region, but did not invite Iran. Naturally, the Iranians saw this as yet another example of U.S. double dealing.

The decision to leave Iran out of the conference was largely due to Israeli pressure. The Israelis had been worried about rapprochement between Iran and the United States. Israel considered Iran a threat not because it was militarily dangerous, but because economically it provided a bigger potential market for U.S. goods and businesses than Israel. The Israelis worried that U.S.-Iran détente would mean Israel would lose its special relationship with the U.S.

Leaving the Iranians out of the regional security apparatus also meant that Iran was free to be the spoiler. Tehran did just that, embarking on a policy to make the U.S. decision to isolate Iran as costly as possible. Many of the problems in the region today stem from the Bush White House's decision to isolate Iran.

After Bush lost his re-election bid and Bill Clinton moved into the Oval Office, not much changed in the adversarial relationship between the two nations. The Israeli government continued to play a large role in preventing the U.S. from reaching out to Iran, convincing the Clinton administration of the need to contain both Iraq's Saddam Hussein and Iran's Islamic government. This policy, known as dual containment, was a shift from previous strategies that sought to balance one with the other.

The Clinton administration had also become preoccupied with the peace process between Israel and Palestine. In an effort to move that forward, the Clinton White House caved to Israeli pressure aimed at targeting Iran. Initially this was in language only, utilizing the now commonplace phrases of "state sponsor of terrorism" and "ardent opponent of the peace process" to describe the Iranian government. But more importantly, Israel pushed for tougher sanctions on Iran.

The Iranians had offered Conoco, an American oil company, a lucrative oil field concession in 1995. It was a significant move, heavy with symbolism. The Clinton administration was aware of the ongoing negotiations between Conoco and the Iranian government. Within a month of the deal being announced, however, the pro-Israel lobby was out in full force in Washington working to squash it. Pressured by this powerful lobby and its allies in Congress, Clinton once again caved to Israeli demands. By issuing two executive orders prohibiting trade with Iran, he essentially snuffed out Conoco's hard-earned deal. Congress, not to be outdone in their anti-Iran efforts, went one step further and codified those executive orders by passing the Iran-Libya Sanctions Act in 1996. The sanctions effectively blocked any effort to improve relations with Iran.

The Iranians were incensed and responded by attacking the Israeli peace process. Tehran began building relationships with Palestinian militant organizations. Since the revolution, Iran had only verbally attacked Israel, never actually following through with their threats. But as Israel spearheaded efforts to isolate Iran, Iranian rhetoric turned to action, further jeopardizing U.S.-Iranian détente.

The 1990s saw hopes of rapprochement dashed by both the Bush and Clinton administrations. Under heavy pro-Israel lobbying and still nursing old wounds from the hostage crisis, both

Democrats and Republicans joined the anti-Iran bandwagon. But it was also in the 1990s that the U.S. and European stances toward Iran began to diverge, with the Europeans favoring détente and economic cooperation. After Congress passed the 1996 Sanctions Act, countries in the European Union protested and continued to do business with Iran.

HOW DID 9/11 AFFECT IRAN'S RELATIONS WITH THE WEST?

The George W. Bush administration had been in office less than eight months in 2001 when the 9/11 terror attacks occurred, attacks that fundamentally changed the region and its relationship with the United States. One might think that 9/11 would have shifted the U.S. alliance from Saudi Arabia to Iran, given that 15 of the 19 hijackers were Saudis and that the attacks were perpetrated by Al Qaeda, a Sunni-based extremist group whose fundamentalist ideology is based on the Saudi's Wahhabist version of Islam. Iran, on the other hand, is a Shia country that had no ties to Al Qaeda.

Moreover, the 9/11 attacks were planned in Afghanistan, where Al Qaeda leadership lived under the protection of the Taliban. Since the mid-1990s, the Iranians had been fighting the Taliban, primarily by assisting their adversaries, the Northern Alliance.

Iranians, both the government and the public, were also very sympathetic towards the United States after the attack. Unlike the celebrations in some Arab nations, where people saw the attacks on the U.S. as a well-deserved blow to Israel's main supporter, Iranians poured into the streets to hold candlelight vigils.[166] Iran's political leaders expressed their condolences and thought the attack might result in a warming of U.S.-Iranians relations. When the Bush administration declared war on the Sunni fundamentalist Taliban regime in Afghanistan that had not only harbored Al Qaeda but had murdered Iranian diplomats, the Iranian government offered assistance. As before, however, the U.S. was reluctant to accept Iran's help, in large part due to continued Israeli pressure.

The U.S. forces invaded Afghanistan, toppled the Taliban from power and pushed Al Qaeda's networks into Pakistan. President Bush then needed a plan to rebuild Afghanistan, and it was here that the Iranians offered assistance. Iran's extensive knowledge of Afghanistan and the connections it had made by backing the anti-Taliban alliance was of enormous help in getting all sides together in Bonn, Germany to try to work out an agreement for an interim government.

James Dobbins, the U.S. special envoy to Afghanistan at the time, described the tense gathering in Bonn, where the disparate factions had reached an impasse. Everything was about to fall apart until the intervention by the Iranian representative Javad Zarif, the same person who 14 years later negotiated the Iran nuclear deal. Zarif talked privately to the Northern Alliance delegate, who then compromised and saved the day. "It was indicative that Iran was collaborating quite constructively with the United States and with the rest of the international community to assure a positive outcome of the conference," Dobbins said.[167]

At the international donors' conference to help rebuild Afghanistan, Iran also played a positive role, pledging a staggering $500 million in assistance—the same amount as the United States. Iran was so eager to continue helping that it even offered to pay to rebuild the Afghan Army, an offer the U.S. refused.[168] Iranian officials were also helpful in extraditing Al Qaeda fighters who had fled Afghanistan and were living in Iran.

Inside the George W. Bush White House, debates were raging about whether to continue collaborating with Iran. The discussions came to a crashing halt when President Bush, in his fateful January 29, 2002 State of the Union address, called Iran part of the "axis of evil."

Bush's speech undercut any movement for positive relations with Iran. Iranian reformists who had lobbied to engage the United States felt betrayed and were throttled by both Bush's rebuke and condemnation from hardliners inside Iran. The opportunity to improve U.S.-Iranian relations in the wake of the 9/11 attacks had been torpedoed by conservative, pro-Israel U.S. politicians.

HOW DID THE 2003 U.S. INVASION OF IRAQ AFFECT RELATIONS?

Then came the U.S.-led invasion of Iraq in March 2003. The Iranian government was delighted to see Saddam Hussein's regime attacked; after all, the Iraqi leader had invaded Iran in 1980 and was responsible for the deaths of hundreds of thousands of Iranians. Iraq was also a majority Shia country where the Shia had been brutally persecuted under Saddam Hussein, and Iran had a long history of supporting its Shia brethren. But the speed with which the U.S. military overthrew Saddam Hussein, doing in three weeks what Iran could not do in eight years of war with Iraq, worried Iran's political leadership. They wanted to make sure that any new Iraqi government would not be a threat to Iran's security.

Initially, Iran held off from sowing seeds of discord. In fact, via Swiss intermediaries, the Iranians sent a proposal to the U.S. State Department laying out the terms of a "grand bargain." It was, in essence, a bold peace treaty that put everything on the table. It offered to negotiate nearly every issue the U.S. had been concerned with—Iran's nuclear program, support for Palestinian militant groups, policy in Iraq, and accepting Israel's right to exist. In return, the U.S. would have to give up hostile behavior towards Iran, end economic sanctions, allow access to peaceful nuclear technology, clampdown on the terrorist group MEK, and acknowledge Iran's security interests.

The Bush administration, elated by its quick victory in defeating Saddam Hussein and believing that regime change in Iran could come next, saw no need to negotiate, and even rebuked the Swiss for playing the role of intermediary. Iran's offer never even received a reply.

The hubris of the Bush officials made them believe their quick success in toppling Saddam Hussein signaled the long-term viability of their agenda to create a new, pro-Western, stable government in Iraq. Instead, their refusal to negotiate with Iran hurt U.S. chances of controlling events on the ground in Iraq. It also sent a message to the hardliners in Iran that the only way to force the United States to treat Iran as a sovereign nation was to be a thorn in its side. That's when Iran began funding, training, and equipping Shia militias inside Iraq.

The first Iraqi election, which took place one year after the U.S. government's pro-consul Paul Bremer had been running the country, put Prime Minister Nouri Maliki in office. Maliki had spent much time in Iran during Saddam Hussein's dictatorship, and his first trip as prime minister was to Tehran. From 2005 onward, successive Iraqi governments have had expensive ties with Iran, much to the consternation of U.S. officials.

HOW DID THE EUROPEANS AFFECT U.S.-IRANIAN NEGOTIATIONS?

In June 2003, just months after the U.S. invasion of Iraq, the U.K., Germany, and France launched a diplomatic effort to address their growing concern about Iran's nuclear policy. The U.S. refused to join the talks. A few months later, the parties reached an agreement known as the Tehran Declaration, where Iran agreed to fully cooperate with the International Atomic Energy Agency (IAEA) and to suspend all uranium enrichment. For the Iranians, they felt the negotiations with the Europeans were a prelude to deeper talks that would include the U.S., but the U.S. was not interested. The buzz phrase in the Bush White House was "we don't talk to evil."[169]

By 2005, the situation had changed. Iraq was a mess, and the Bush administration finally decided that engaging Iran was worth a shot. Rather than recognize that Iran had already suspended uranian enrichment, however, the White House demanded that Iran give up fuel production altogether as a precondition for talks. The Iranians refused.

In the meantime, presidential elections in Iran were looming. Western governments were hopeful that former President Hashemi Rafsanjani, a reformist, would win. They did not bank on the conservative former Tehran mayor Mahmoud Ahmadinejad edging out Rafsanjani. Reformists had stuck their necks out on multiple occasions to build a more positive relationship with the United States. In return, the U.S. had shut the door or ignored their overtures. With Ahmadinejad in office, whatever political capital the reformists still had soon evaporated. Now the hardliners had the green light.

Almost immediately after Ahmadinejad took office, Iran restarted its suspended nuclear program. By mid-2006, after a failed attempt at restarting negotiations, the Germans stepped in and persuaded the Bush administration to try again. The Germans realized there would not be any long-term solution without U.S. involvement, but Bush's team once again insisted that the suspension of uranium enrichment was a precondition. For the Iranians, this was a non-starter. They had already suspended their program once and received nothing in return.

The Bush administration was surprised Iran said "no," but it should not have been. In the waning days of the second Bush White House, Iran's nuclear program was gaining ground, and it was clear Iran would also gain from the chaos in Iraq. Bush had, through his own hubris, neutered America's ability to build a consensus around Iran. It took the election of a new U.S. president for that to be rebuilt.

WHAT DID OBAMA'S 'UNCLENCHED FIST' DIPLOMATIC INITIATIVE DO TO IMPROVE RELATIONS?

In November 2008, the United States elected Barack Obama, who had promised to improve America's relations with the rest of the world, especially the Middle East. His approach extended to Iran as well. After 12 years of American failure to recognize openings, Obama's election was a breath of fresh air and a time of hope.

Almost immediately after taking office in late January 2009, President Obama sent clear signals that he sought to engage the Iranians, both private citizens and the government. Just a few weeks after taking office, President Obama sent a video message to the Iranian people for the Persian New Year, Nowruz.[170] It was intended to show the Iranians that Obama appreciated their culture and understood the importance of hospitality and respect. The Iranians were appreciative of his message.

Progress on any diplomatic initiative was muted, though, because of the pending Iranian presidential elections in June 2009, in which conservative President Ahmadinejad was vying for another term. The Obama administration had hoped that someone more amenable to diplomatic efforts would be elected. They almost got their wish with challenger Mir-Hossein Mousavi. On election day, the two were neck and neck, but the official results gave Ahmadinejad a landslide victory. The public cried foul.

In the ensuing days and weeks, protests raged across the country. The movement for a recount and for more transparency became known as the Green Movement. International media outlets endlessly covered the unfolding events, but as time progressed the Iranian government was determined to move forward with Ahmadinejad as president. Instead of letting the protests die out, they decided to violently crack down on citizens who had taken to the streets.

The Obama administration had hoped to jumpstart diplomatic efforts after the election was over. Now they were scrambling to figure out how to respond to the protests. Obama wanted to support the Green Movement but did not want to eliminate the possibility of future engagement with the government. Conservatives in the U.S. Congress called for more sanctions and more public support for the Green Movement. Ironically, the movement did not want open support from the U.S. government, as such support would jeopardize the legitimacy of the opposition.[171]

Several months later, however, Obama sought to engage the Iranian government regarding their nuclear program. Over a series of meetings, diplomats from the five permanent members of the UN Security Council (the U.S., UK, France, Russia, and China) plus Germany (P5+1) met with Iranian officials to deal with Iran's low enriched uranium stockpile. If Iran could enrich it further, the stockpile would be enough to reach the highly enriched uranium necessary for a nuclear weapon. A complex proposal involving shipments between Russia, France, and Iran had traction, but a deal was never reached.

Frustrated, the Obama administration set a different course. Rather than trying to engage Iran, the White House doggedly pursued building a consensus among the P5+1 to impose even tougher sanctions. The Chinese and Russians were initially reluctant, but after months of negotiations and Iran's intransigence, they agreed to support new UN Security Council sanctions.

Just as the UN Security Council was debating new sanctions, two upstart countries, Turkey and Brazil, tried to give diplomacy another chance. After getting tepid approval from the Obama administration, Turkish and Brazilian diplomats went to Iran to re-engage on the nuclear issue. [172] To everyone's surprise, they were successful in getting an agreement that essentially mirrored what had been discussed six months earlier. Iran would exchange a portion of its low enriched uranium for fuel pads. Only this time, the deal was too little too late. The Obama administration scuttled the new deal, because Iran's enriched uranium stockpile had nearly doubled, and international consensus had already been built around a new set of sanctions. That little glimmer of hope created by Turkey and Brazil was snuffed out by the United States.

Sanctions on Iran passed the UN Security Council, and for the next two years, as the U.S. turned up the pressure on Iran, the two countries were locked in a stalemate over the nuclear issue. Iran accelerated its program, increasing stockpiles of enriched uranium and increasing the number of centrifuges. Both countries engaged in tit-for-tat cyberattacks on each other's infrastructure. And in early 2012, the U.S. Congress passed sanctions on Iran's Central Bank, which essentially cut Iran off from participating in global commerce.

Around the same time as the banking sanctions, new rounds of talks were starting with a secret back channel via the government of Oman.[173] Over the course of the next year, the secret talks would continue building trust, but no agreement.

When Hassan Rouhani became Iran's new president in June 2013, new life was breathed into the back channel. President

Obama had been forced to reconsider his position on zero enrichment. There was pressure from the Omanis and Europeans, as well as recognition that the sanctions were having a diminishing impact. All the while, Iran's nuclear program was advancing.

As the back channel continued to hammer out a framework for enrichment, inspections, and removal of sanctions, the P5+1 renewed its meetings as well. In November 2013 they reached an interim agreement and tried to hash out the final sticking points, including the future of a heavy water reactor at Natanz, the release of Iranian frozen assets held in U.S. banks, and limitations on enrichment and research bans.

The global public watched with bated breath, as deadlines kept getting extended. At several moments it seemed that the entire deal would collapse, as each side threatened to walk away. Finally, after a 12-year-standoff, 20 months of on-and-off talks, and a final 17-day marathon round of uninterrupted negotiations, an historic deal was reached on July 14, 2015.

Then came the next step: a Herculean effort by both the Obama administration and the grassroots organizations to get the necessary congressional approval. Despite heavy lobbying by the pro-Israel organization AIPAC (American Israeli Public Affairs Committee) and other lobby groups created specifically to quash the deal, Congress failed to block the agreement, giving victory to a hard-fought diplomatic battle.

Negotiations were also taking place regarding a different issue: a prisoner swap. Several Iranian-American dual nationals were being held in Iranian prisons, most notably *Washington Post* journalist Jason Rezaian. In exchange for their release, the U.S. agreed to release several Iranians held in American jails. Adding to the complexity was the fact that several U.S. sailors, after a series of mistakes and navigation equipment malfunctions, had drifted into Iranian waters and were detained by the Iranian

MEDEA BENJAMIN

Revolutionary Guard's Navy. Leaning on the already good rapport between Secretary of State John Kerry and Iranian Foreign Minister Javad Zarif, the sailors were released after 16 hours.

The U.S. and Iran had figured out a diplomatic solution to the nuclear impasse and the trust they had built allowed them to hammer out other agreements. But the two countries remained at odds over many issues, including Iran's role in the unrest in Iraq and Syria. Another concern was Iran's continued testing of missiles, even though this was not directly prohibited under the nuclear accords.

As the Obama administration prepared to leave office, hopes were high that the next president would build on his efforts. Both countries had gone a long way to establish trust and institutionalize their interactions. What they did not anticipate, however, was Donald Trump becoming the next president.

WILL TRUMP'S "MAKE AMERICA GREAT AGAIN" LEAD US TO A FAMILIAR PATH?

Riding a wave of right-wing populism, Donald Trump was elected to replace Barack Obama. He promised to bring jobs back, renegotiate trade deals that hurt Americans, and—notably—tear up the Iran nuclear deal that he called the "worst deal ever negotiated."[174]

Despite Iran's compliance with the terms of the agreement, President Trump insisted on the contrary. On October 13, 2017, Trump dealt a blow to the pact by refusing to certify that Iran was in compliance with the accord, despite all evidence by U.S. and international specialists that Iran had compiled. If the U.S. abandons the nuclear accord, the other P5+1 countries have said they would remain committed to it. What Trump is risking, however, is that Iran will say the deal has been violated and restart its enrichment program.[175] We could be in for a long road of increased instability and conflict in an already tumultuous region.

WHY HAVE U.S. POLICYMAKERS BEEN SO SUPPORTIVE OF THE MEK?

In 1997, the MEK (People's Mujahedeen of Iran) was listed by the United States as a terrorist group. Indeed, it has a sordid history of violent attacks, first against the Shah and U.S. businessmen in Iran, and later against the Islamic Republic once it fell out of favor with Ayatollah Khomeini. MEK members were early examples of suicide bombers, strapping themselves with explosives and blowing up civilians in Iran. Israel used the MEK to penetrate Iran and assassinate nuclear scientists. The MEK also took their attacks overseas, targeting Iranian diplomatic missions in 13 countries.

The MEK is a cult-like organization run by Massoud Rajavi and his wife Maryam. A 1994 State Department report documented how Massoud Rajavi "fostered a cult of personality around himself that had alienated most Iranian expatriates, who assert they do not want to replace one objectionable regime for another." A 2009 Rand study described the group as having "cultic practices," including mandatory divorce and celibacy, because "love for the Rajavis was to replace love for spouses and family." In 2013, a George Mason University study found that only five percent of Iranians showed any support for the MEK.[176]

In the United States, however, the group launched a hard-core lobbying campaign to get itself off the terrorist list and rehabilitate itself as a legitimate opposition to the Iranian regime. It has large sums of money for the campaign, reportedly coming from Israel, Saudi Arabia, and a handful of wealthy Iranian-Americans.

Their campaign became a classic case in how to buy influence in Washington DC. The MEK used its funds to secure the backing of an astounding array of U.S. politicians across the political spectrum—from liberal Democrat Howard Dean to conservative Republican Newt Gingrich. It gathered support from pro-Israel figures, including Holocaust survivor Elie Wiesel and Harvard law professor Alan Dershowitz.[177]

Many of its high-profile advocates—including members of Congress, Washington lobby groups, and influential former officials— received large contributions for their support.[178] The funds were disbursed as speaker and lobby fees, campaign contributions, and expensive travel reimbursements. The MEK paid up to $100,000 for people to make public appearances at their events.

As the *New York Times* noted, "Rarely in the annals of lobbying in the capital has so obscure a cause attracted so stellar a group of supporters: former directors of the CIA and the FBI, retired generals and famous politicians of both parties."[179]

Their campaign worked. In 2012, Secretary of State Hillary Clinton announced that the MEK had been removed from the State Department's list of terrorist organizations.

While the MEK continues to have many supporters within Congress and a large pool of big name advocates, a group that fought alongside Saddam Hussein in the Iran-Iraq war, has ties to the CIA and Israel's Mossad, and functions in a cult-like manner is hard pressed to be a viable alternative to Iran's present government. The group might have been able to buy support in the U.S. capital, but it has virtually zero support inside Iran.

CHAPTER 9: IRAN IN THE MIDDLE EAST AND BEYOND

With the Middle East on fire, Iran is certainly involved in many of the region's conflicts. As a Shia nation in a predominantly Sunni region, and a Persian country in an Arab world, Iran has felt surrounded by threats. Iran is the Muslim country in the Middle East that has been most adamantly opposed to radical Sunni terrorist groups, from the Taliban to Al Qaeda to ISIS. Iran has been fighting all of those groups in other countries in the region, somehow managing—for the most part—to keep the fighting away from its own homeland.

That's why Iranians were so shocked by an unprecedented terrorist attack in June 2017 in the heart of Tehran, hitting the Parliament and the mausoleum of Ayatollah Khomeini. Seventeen people were killed and dozens injured. ISIS took credit for the attack, which seems to have been carried out by disaffected Iranian Kurds.[180] Iran sees all of these fanatical Sunni groups as being nurtured, in one way or another, by the Wahhabists in Saudi Arabia. It is one more reason why Iran's relations with the rest of the world have to be filtered through the lens of its intense hostility with Saudi Arabia, and to a lesser extent with the United States and Israel.

WHAT'S BEHIND THE SAUDI/IRAN RIVALRY?

Saudi leaders see Iran's post-1979 policies as part of an expansionist, sectarian agenda aimed at empowering Shia Muslims in the region at the expense of Sunnis. Iranian leaders attribute similar motives to their Saudi counterparts.

It wasn't always this way. The religious division between Sunni and Shia dates back to the religion's founding in the seventh century, but Sunni and Shia have coexisted without significant conflict for much of the history of the Middle East.

With the 1979 Islamic Revolution, the initial message of the Iranian leader, Ayatollah Khomeini, was not only anti-imperialist but anti-monarchy. He claimed that Islam was incompatible with hereditary monarchies. Khomeini tried to position himself as the leader of all Muslims, regardless of their denomination. In doing so, he challenged the legitimacy of the Saudi royal family and called into question its status as guardian of Islam's two holy sites, Mecca and Medina. The Saudi rulers' response was to denounce Iran's revolution as a power play by heretical Shiites.

In essence, the Saudi–Iran rivalry is not religious, but political. When Shah Pahlavi ruled Iran from 1941 to 1979, the two nations had a decent relationship. Both were original members of the oil cartel OPEC. The problem between the two countries arose when revolutionary religious leaders in Iran posed an ideological threat to the Saudi regime.

During the Iran–Iraq war in the 1980s, Saudi Arabia took the side of Saddam Hussein's Iraq as a way to weaken Iran. This caused tremendous anger among Iranians.

Relations were further strained in 1987, when 275 Iranians died at the hands of Saudi police during a pilgrimage to Mecca. While in Mecca, the Iranians had organized, as they did every year, a demonstration against the United States and Israel. This time, however, they were brutally attacked by Saudi riot police. In response, protesters in Iran occupied the Saudi Embassy and a Saudi diplomat died when he fell out of an embassy window.

Saudi Arabia severed relations with Iran in 1988; they were later restored in 1991.

Relations improved in the late 1990s, when Saudi Crown Prince Abdullah visited Iran in 1997, followed by an official visit to Saudi Arabia by Iranian reformist President Mohammad Khatami the following year. The 2003 U.S. invasion of Iraq, however, led to more turmoil. The power vacuum created by the overthrow of Saddam Hussein and disastrous U.S. policies, such as firing hundreds of thousands of Sunnis in the ruling Baath Party, unleashed fierce infighting between Iraq's Sunni and Shia communities. Iran supported Iraqi Shia; Saudi Arabia supported Iraqi Sunnis.

The enmity between Saudi Arabia and Iran became even fiercer eight years later, in 2011, with the Arab Spring. As some regimes were toppled and others desperately clung to power, the Saudis and Iranians competed for influence and dominance. By 2016, the Saudis accused Iran of waging proxy wars in Iraq, Syria, Yemen, Bahrain, Kuwait, and even inside the kingdom itself; Iran viewed Saudi Arabia as destabilizing the entire Middle East. While many of the claims were false or exaggerated, both countries had a hand in the regional conflicts.

Another area of tension was Iran's nuclear program. The Saudis seemed to be less concerned about Iran's nuclear ambitions than the possibility that a deal would bring Iran back into the international fold and threaten the cozy U.S.–Saudi alliance. The Saudis eventually gave a nod of approval for the deal when President Obama pledged more weapons sales to Saudi Arabia and beefed up military support to defend itself against potential missile strikes, maritime threats, and cyberattacks from Iran.

In September 2015, hundreds of Iranians were killed in a stampede during the annual Hajj pilgrimage in Mecca, Saudi Arabia. Iran accused the Saudis of gross negligence and mismanagement, and Saudi officials accused Iran of playing politics in the aftermath of a tragedy.

Another bone of contention has been Iran's connection with dissident Shia groups in eastern Saudi Arabia and Bahrain (where Shia are the majority). The Shia populations in both countries have been oppressed, and Iran has occasionally entered the fray to offer support.

Relations between the two nations came to a breaking point in 2016, when Saudi Arabia executed anti-government activist and Shiite cleric Nimr al-Nimr on trumped-up charges of terrorism. The killing of the nonviolent sheikh, beloved by the Shia community at home and abroad, predictably outraged many Shia in Iran. They staged violent protests at the Saudi Embassy in Tehran, including setting it on fire. Saudi Arabia cut off all diplomatic and economic ties with Iran.

Saudi Arabia and Iran were also on opposite sides in the conflicts in Syria and then in Yemen. They came close to direct confrontation after Saudi Arabia held Iran responsible for a ballistic missile fired from Yemen on November 4, 2017 that landed near the airport in Saudi's capital city Riyadh.

When Donald Trump became president in 2017, he exacerbated tensions by publicly cozying up to the Saudis, continuing to sell them weapons, and expanding U.S. support for the Yemen war. Emboldened by U.S. support—and with power in the hands of the rash, young Crown Prince Mohammad bin Salman—Saudi Arabia stepped up its actions to isolate Iran.

HOW DOES IRAN RELATE TO THE OTHER GULF COUNTRIES?

In 1981, against the backdrop of the Iranian revolution and the Iran-Iraq war, the Gulf States banded together to form the Gulf

Cooperation Council (GCC). It was composed of the six Arab monarchies in the Persian Gulf: Saudi Arabia, Bahrain, Kuwait, Oman, Qatar, and the United Arab Emirates (UAE). De facto leadership of the GCC was in the hands of Saudi Arabia.

While the GCC countries have many common interests, ranging from trade to ensuring that their monarchies remain intact to promoting Sunni dominance in the region, the GCC is not a monolith. Tensions can be high within that organization as well, as happened in 2017 when Saudi Arabia and a few other nations broke off diplomatic relations with GCC member Qatar. Kuwait and Oman refused to go along with Saudi demands.

One of the reasons for the Saudi decision to isolate Qatar was that Qatar, despite opposing Iran in the conflicts in Syria and Yemen, openly advocated for better relations with Iran. Qatar and Iran share control over the vast South Pars/North Dome oil and natural gas field. The field sits offshore and northeast of Qatar and just south of Iran. The Iranians have been slow to exploit the enormous offshore resources, but the shared resource is a major incentive for Qatar to maintain positive relations with Iran.

Qatar, a tiny nation with enormous wealth thanks to natural gas, refused to comply with the Saudi demand that it cut ties with Iran. The Saudis responded with a blockade. This move, however, only pushed Qatar and Iran closer together since Iran stepped in to supply whatever imports Qatar needed and allowed Qatar Airlines to fly over Iranian territory so the airlines could continue its routes to Europe and Asia.

Other GCC states have business ties to Iran as well. This includes Kuwait, with its large Iranian expat population. Iran's largest GCC economic partner is Dubai, one of the United Arab Emirates. During the Iran-Iraq War, while most of the GCC countries sided with Iraq, Dubai allowed Iran to use its territory for resupplying its military. Prior to the imposition of hard-hitting sanctions in 2012, trade between Dubai and Iran accounted for nearly 25 percent of Iran's international trade. After a 2009 financial crisis and bailout from another UAE emirate, Abu Dhabi, Dubai caved to external pressure and began rolling back trade with Iran. But as Iran's economy picked back up after the 2015 signing of the nuclear deal, Dubai became the main beneficiary in the Gulf.

Iran has maintained close ties with the Gulf state of Oman. Before the Iranian revolution, Iran helped the Sultan of Oman fight off a rebellion, and after the revolution, they continued to have positive relations. At times, Oman serves as the interlocutor for countries dealing with Iran. This was the case when U.S. and Iranian officials held secret talks starting in 2011 regarding Iran's nuclear program.

There are also some ongoing territorial disputes with Iran that strain regional relations. The UAE has laid claim to three islands Iran has occupied prior to the revolution. Iran does not acknowledge the UAE's claim.

HOW CAN THE RELATIONSHIP WITH ISRAEL BE DEFINED?

It's hard to imagine two more bitter enemies than Iran and Israel, with Iranian leaders calling for Israel's demise and Israeli leaders calling Iran an existential threat to Israel. Yet this animosity is relatively new. Before Iran's 1979 revolution, the two nations were allies. Iranian diplomats in Europe saved thousands of Jews from the Holocaust. Although the Shah voted against 1947 Partition Plan for Palestine at the end of the British Mandate, rightly asserting that it would lead to violence, Iran was still the second Muslim-majority country to formally recognize Israel.

Iran and Israel saw each other as natural regional allies, in large part due to their non-Arab backgrounds and their common Sunni

Arab enemies. The two nations shared intelligence and weapons. Their ties were further cemented through various joint ventures and robust trade. Both were closely allied with the United States.

Iran remained neutral in all three Arab-Israeli wars. Even during the Arab oil boycott of the 1970s, Iran continued to supply Israel with oil. Iran's population of some 100,000 Jews was another factor tying the nations together.

After the 1979 revolution, the relationship did an about-face. Iran's new rulers viewed Israel as an American lackey and denounced Israel's suppression of Palestinian rights. But even though the rhetoric was heated, Israel continued to supply arms to Iran during the Iran/Iraq war and Israel served as a middleman during the Reagan administration's arms-for-hostages deal.

As the Iran-Iraq war ended, Iran stepped up its support for Hezbollah in Lebanon and formed new alliances with Palestinian militias. Through funding and training of Palestinian militants, Iran played a role in several bombing attacks inside Israel, as well as the bombing of the Israeli Embassy and a Jewish Center in Argentina.

The staunchest ally of the Palestinians in the region, however, was Iraq's Saddam Hussein. Iraq had declared war on the Jewish state in 1948, sent armies to fight Israel in 1948, 1968, and 1973, and subsidized families of Palestinian martyrs (including suicide bombers). When the 1991 Gulf War severely weakened Saddam Hussein, the Israelis swtiched to identifying Iran as their major threat in the region. Israel used its close relationship with the U.S. to lobby for isolating Iran. Israel pushed for increased sanctions and in 1995 was responsible for scuttling a major oil deal between Iran and the U.S. oil company Conoco.

After the U.S. invaded and occupied Iraq, the Iranians offered up a grand bargain in which they indicated they would be open to recognizing Israel's right to exist, but their offer never received a response.

In the 2000s, Iran's nuclear program became an even bigger focus for the Israelis, despite the fact that Israel had illegally developed its own nuclear weapons and refused to sign onto the Nuclear Non-Proliferation Treaty.

Israel seized on every new Iranian effort to develop and protect its nuclear industry, such as the discovery of its Natanz underground uranium enrichment site in 2002, as evidence that Iran would have a nuclear bomb within a few years.

As Trita Parsi documented in his book, *A Single Roll of the Dice: Obama's Diplomacy with Iran*, President Obama's "dual-track" approach to Iran's nuclear program during his first term was a political compromise between hawks and doves in Washington. The hawks, who were allied with Netanyahu and the Israel lobby, were determined to destroy Iran's nuclear program by crippling sanctions or even by war. The doves wanted to avoid war with Iran and resolve the nuclear scare through diplomacy.

The Obama administration was also dogged by the fear that Israel would follow through on its threats to take matters into its own hands by launching a unilateral strike on Iran's nuclear program. The fact that Israel had done this twice before, in Iraq and Syria, gave the threats more credence. Iran's allies, including Hezbollah and Hamas, would surely have responded by striking deep inside Israeli territory. It was clear any attack by Israel would likely pull the U.S. into yet another regional conflict.[181]

Israel vigorously opposed the Iran nuclear deal, directly lobbying the White House and Congress, including getting the Republican congressional leadership to give Israeli Prime Minister Netanyahu an unprecedented invitation to speak about Israel's opposition to the nuclear agreement to a 2015 joint session of Congress without even informing the White House of the invitation.

Israel was also implicated in a more brutal tactic to oppose the nuclear deal: the assassination of nuclear scientists inside Iran.

Between 2010 and 2012, at least five scientists associated with Iran's nuclear program were killed. Darioush Rezaeinejad, an electrical engineer, was killed by gunmen on motorcycles in July 2011. Mostafa Ahmadi Rosham, deputy head of Iran's nuclear enrichment program, was killed in January 2012 by a bomb attached to his car door—also by men on motorcycles.[182] While these assassinations were not directly attributed to Israel, strong evidence points in that direction. NBC reported that U.S. officials, speaking off-record, claimed Israel's Mossad had trained Iranian exiles from the MEK for the assassination campaign.[183] Israeli Defense Minister Moshe Ya'alon did not explicitly deny Israeli responsibility, instead ominously claiming he bore no responsibility "for the life expectancy of Iranian scientists," and that Israel would "act in any way" to prevent a nuclear-armed Iran.[184]

When the nuclear deal was finally negotiated in 2015 and was received with near unanimous international consensus, Israel was the outlier with its condemnation of the agreement.

Iran's involvement in Syria has also caused concern for Israel. The successful effort by Russia, Iran, and Hezbollah to prop up the Assad regime meant stronger, better equipped, Iranian-backed militias on Israel's borders with both Lebanon and Syria. Israel saw the spread of Iranian-backed militias to Syria as a serious shift in the military balance on its borders, which is why it launched several airstrikes in Syria against them and quietly supported the Al Qaeda-linked forces the Iranians were fighting.

In its efforts to push back against Iran, Israel found an odd bedfellow: Saudi Arabia. With the old adage that "the enemy of my enemy is my friend," the Israelis made common cause with Saudi Arabia, the only country in the Middle East where it would be illegal to build a synagogue.

WHAT DEFINES IRAN'S RELATIONSHIP WITH OTHER NEIGHBORS ON ITS BORDERS?

Not only does Iran have to navigate turbulent relations with GCC countries that sit along its 1,500 mile coastline on the Persian Gulf, but it must also traverse an equally stormy set of relationships with seven other neighbors with whom it shares 3,300 miles of borders: Afghanistan, Armenia, Azerbaijan, Iraq, Pakistan, Turkey and Turkmenistan.

These countries, at some point in their histories, have been part of one of the various Persian empires. Travelers will often find cultural, social, and linguistic commonalities in these countries based on centuries-old contact. But today's relations are forged through a complex blend of wars, sanctions, religious identities, ideology, shifting alliances, and economic interests. Each relationship is unique, and fluctuates according to the breathtaking pace and scope of changes that have been taking place in the region.

IRAQ

Iran's longest border is the one with Iraq—over 900 miles long. Historically, that border has been porous, due in large part to extensive cross-border trade and tourism. Every year, hundreds of thousands of Iranians make pilgrimages to Shia religious shrines in Najaf and Karbala in southern Iraq. This geographic closeness, along with the fact that both Iran and Iraq are majority Shia, means that the two nations are, for better or worse, inextricably linked.

Relations were tense before the Iranian revolution, with the Shah trying to organize a coup against Saddam Hussein in 1971 and Saddam Hussein supporting insurgencies against the Shah. But the real catastrophe came in 1980, when Iraq invaded Iran, sparking an eight-year war that left over a million dead and wounded.

After the ceasefire with Iraq, Iran continued to play host to several Iraqi Shia dissident groups. These groups would end up forming the core of Iran's influence in Iraq for decades to come.

When the U.S. decided to invade Iraq in 2003, Iran was hesitant to get involved. The ensuing chaos brought on by the U.S. occupation and Baathist insurgency forced Iran's hand. Using its extensive network of Shia dissident groups, the Iranians fought both the U.S. occupying forces and the Iraqi army.

Despite the massive American presence, it was the Iranians who played kingmaker in Iraq. Iraq's Shia militias and political leaders coalesced around the new Iranian-backed leadership. All three Iraqi prime ministers since 2006 owed their positions to Iranian influence, and ironically, Iran owed its influence to the U.S. overthrow of Saddam Hussein.

After the U.S. withdrew its troops in 2011 and ISIS (formed primarily by men who had been imprisoned in Iraq by U.S. forces) grabbed control over swaths of western and northern Iraq, Iran re-mobilized the Shia militias it had controlled during the U.S. occupation. Iranian-backed militias fought alongside the Iraqi Army and Kurdish Peshmerga to push ISIS out of Iraq.

Once ISIS was defeated by the end of 2017, however, Shia militias joined the Iraqi Army to confront their former allies, the Peshmerga, and push the Kurds out of the northern, oil-rich city of Kirkuk.

While U.S. officials deny it, the fight against ISIS in Iraq involved a tacit U.S. alliance with Iran. A coalition of mainly Shia Iraqi militias, known as the Popular Mobilization Units (PMUs), were officially formed in 2014 and were key to defeating ISIS. U.S. officials fear that these Shia militias, even though they are technically part of the Iraqi Armed Forces, will eventually become much like Hezbollah or even the Iranian Revolutionary Guard—armed Shia groups independent of the official military, ready to do Iran's bidding.

But there are limits to Iran's influence. The U.S. has been pressing the Iraqi leaders to send Iranian fighters home and minimize Iran's power. There is also tremendous resentment among the sizable Sunni population in Iraq, some of whom have been terrorized by Shia militia for years.

The Iraqi leaders know they are walking a tightrope, trying to please both their American patrons and their Iranian allies. To keep control, defeat Sunni extremist groups, and prevent the total breakaway of Iraqi Kurdistan, Iraqi leaders are aware they need both the Iranians and the Americans. So far, they have been brilliantly playing the two off each other.

There is no doubt, however, that the U.S. overthrow of Iran's archrival in Iraq, Saddam Hussein, turned out not only to be a catastrophe for Iraqis, but for the Sunni-Shia sectarian violence it unleashed that opened the door for Iran to play a major role in the future of Iraq.

AFGHANISTAN

Iran's eastern neighbor, Afghanistan, has experienced 40 years of coups and wars, including the longest war ever waged by the United States. Iran's influence has mainly been along the border in the western, mostly Tajik, Farsi-speaking city and province of Herat, which is sometimes referred to as "Little Iran." Most Afghan Tajiks are Sunni Muslims, but both Hazaras and a Tajik minority called the Farsiwan are Shia, giving them another link with Iran. During the Soviet invasion in the 1980s, two million Afghans fled and took refuge in Iran.

With the emergence of the Taliban government in 1996 and its harsh treatment of Afghan minorities, Iran refused to recognize the Taliban and instead provided military support to the

Tajik-majority Northern Alliance opposition. Relations further deteriorated in 1998, when the Taliban attacked the Iranian consulate in Afghanistan, killing ten diplomats and a journalist. Iran's support for the Northern Alliance helped the United States topple the Taliban in 2001. When the various anti-Taliban forces came together to negotiate the post-Taliban peace, Iran's links with the Northern Alliance were the key to getting all sides to come to an agreement. Iran was also set to play a larger role in the post-Taliban reconstruction of Afghanistan until President George W. Bush decided to take a hostile stance against Iran.

Iran says its goal in Afghanistan is to have a stable country on its border, which means eliminating the Taliban and Al Qaeda. It wants a greater focus on drug trafficking. Afghanistan is the world's largest source of opium, and Iran is the main conduit for international traffickers to get the drugs out to Europe. The trafficking through Iran has created a chronic drug problem in Iran, and hundreds of Iranian security agents have been killed in clashes with drug traffickers.

Over the years, Iran has spent hundreds of millions of dollars in reconstruction investments in Afghanistan, including the building of a railroad to the western city of Herat. It has spearheaded an ambitious, politically charged project to connect Afghanistan to the Iranian port of Chabahar, creating a route that would significantly shorten the distance between Afghanistan and the Persian Gulf and compete with the traditional roadway through Pakistan.

A major Iranian goal in Afghanistan, however, is to see that U.S. troops leave; Iran does not want American soldiers on its border. With the Trump administration upping troop numbers and military involvement in Afghanistan, Iran has been trying to undermine the U.S. presence.

Some reports allege that Iran's strategy includes support for the Taliban in their attacks on US forces, which the Iranian government denies. Major support for the Afghan Taliban still comes from Pakistan. Iran insists that its contacts with the Taliban have only been to encourage them to pursue peace talks rather than continue their military activities.[185]

Both the United States and Iran are worried about a new development in Afghanistan: the presence of ISIS groups. A mini-caliphate was established in 2017 in the province of Jawzjan, started by disaffected Taliban elements and fighters streaming out from Iraq and Syria.[186] Given the ISIS attacks that took place in the heart of Iran in June 2017, Iran's leaders are determined to make sure that Afghanistan does not become a haven for ISIS fighters.

Moreover, while the war in Afghanistan is the longest in U.S. history, the Iranians are convinced that, at some point, the U.S. military will get tired and go home. Iran, Afghanistan's next door neighbor, will remain and will continue to use its influence with successive Afghan governments.

TURKEY

Turkey and Iran are descendants of historic empires that share geographic, ethnic, and linguistic ties. Their relationship in modern times has been mainly peaceful, but often tense and suspicious.

After the 1979 Iranian revolution, relations remained cool even though Turkey supplied Iran with much-needed goods during the Iran-Iraq war. The main flash point early on was the religious-secular divide, with Turkey being a constitutionally secular state before the ascent of Recep Tayyip Erdogan's Islamist party in 2002. There were also concerns over support for separatist groups, particularly Kurds, within each country. Turkey's membership in NATO brought U.S. troops to Iran's borders, which made Iran nervous.[187]

The rise of Erdogan's Justice and Development Party (AKP) in 2002 and his "zero problems with neighbors" policy saw relations start to warm. At the behest of the Turkish government, Iran even reduced its contacts with the Kurdish groups it had previously supported. And in 2010, Erdogan—along with Brazilian President Lula da Silva—spearheaded an effort to find an international solution to the nuclear impasse with Iran.

Just a year later, tensions flared as Iran and Turkey found themselves on opposite sides during the Arab Spring. The worst flashpoint was Syria. Turkey was determined to see Bashar al-Assad toppled; Iran was determined to see his government survive. Iran accused Turkey of being the supply source for ISIS in the region, and Turkey said Iran's role in supporting Assad was irresponsible.[188]

The two countries found themselves with mutual interests, however, when the Saudis boycotted Qatar in 2017. Both Iran and Turkey came to Qatar's aid, and trade among the three countries increased.[189]

Bilateral trade between Iran and Turkey is focused on the energy sector. Iran has significant oil and gas reserves, but due to sanctions has trouble exploiting them. Turkey has money and access to technology. In the future, ties on that front will likely improve if Turkish companies can find ways to avoid becoming embroiled in U.S. sanctions on Iranian industries.

PAKISTAN

While Iran's relationship with Turkey has improved, its relationship with Pakistan has soured. Pakistan is a Sunni-majority country with a large Shia population. Prior to the revolution, the two countries were close—Iran was quick to reach out to Pakistan when Pakistan became a nation in 1947.

Multiple fissures emerged after the 1979 Iranian revolution. First, Pakistan became home to Sunni extremists. General Zia-ul-Haq, who had seized power in Pakistan in 1977 and imposed sharia law, was a staunch follower of Sunni Islam and strengthened ties with the Saudis. He gave the Saudis free rein to create Islamic schools across the country to fill the gap of a collapsed education system. Flush with cash from soaring oil prices, the Saudis funded schools and mosques to teach their Wahhabi extremist version of Sunni Islam, an ideology that paints Shia as infidels. This exacerbated the Sunni-Shia sectarian divide, both in Pakistan and beyond its borders, hurting relations with Iran.

Second, Pakistan and Iran conflict over trade. Both countries are anxious to connect Central Asia to international markets. Pakistan already provides Afghanistan with overland access, but Iran is planning an alternative to bypass the Pakistani route. Iran's plans to link Kandahar, Afghanistan, with Iran's new port at Chabahar could put Pakistan's trade route out of business, primarily because the road is shorter and safer than the one in Pakistan.

To make matters worse, Pakistan's adversary, India, is helping Iran develop the Chabahar port. Pakistan views this and other Indian investments in Iran as part of an Indian plot to encircle and isolate Pakistan. At the same time, Pakistan's strong economic ties with Saudi Arabia are threatening to Iran.

Third, border issues have led to finger pointing on both sides. Iran blames Pakistan for the rise of Sunni militancy along Iran's southeast border. Iran's southeast is also restless due to a Baluchi insurgency, which is funded by illicit trading and drug smuggling. Iran has called for greater cooperation with Pakistan to counter smuggling, trafficking, and Baluchi separatist groups.[190]

AZERBAIJAN, ARMENIA, AND TURKMENISTAN

The Azeri, Armenian, and Turkmen peoples were all part of Iran or the Iranian Empire for many centuries, but large parts of their historic territories were conquered by Russia during the expansion of the Russian Empire in the 18th and 19th centuries.

When the Soviet Union broke up at the end of the Cold War, the Soviet parts of these territories became independent countries, while other parts remained within the borders of Iran and other countries in the region. Roughly 55 percent of the world's Azeri population, 22 percent of Turkmen, and two percent of Armenians still live in Iran.

Ties with Azerbaijan should, on the surface, be strong. Both countries are Shia and have a shared history, as well as cultural and linguistic ties. Most of the world's Azeris live in Iran, not in Azerbaijan. But after a brief, positive relationship after the fall of the Soviet Union in the early 1990s, the two countries have spent the intervening years viewing each other with intense suspicion.[191]

Azerbaijan, a secular state anxious to disentangle itself from Russia, sought cooperation with the West, making Iran wary of a pro-Western country on its border. When the Azeris in Azerbaijan decided to advocate for reunification with the Azeri portion of Iran, Tehran began supporting Azerbaijan's bitter rival, Armenia, during their clash over the disputed territory of Nagorno-Karabakh.

Azerbaijan has been gaining influence internationally, mostly due to increased revenues from oil and gas. A deeper treasury has brought them new trading partners. In 2012, to the consternation of Iran, they signed a $1.6 billion military agreement with Israel. Around the same time, the Azerbaijani government claimed it broke up an Iranian cell that had planned to attack the Israeli Embassy in Azerbaijan.

More recently, however, the two sides have moved closer. Energy and transport links have increased, and in October 2017, Iran, Russia, and Azerbaijan met to discuss a framework to strengthen trilateral ties.

Iran's relations with Azerbaijan's neighbor, Armenia, have remained cordial. Iran's large Christian Armenian population is influential, despite different religious preferences. Iran has viewed Armenia as a gateway to Western markets.[192]

With respect to Turkmenistan, Iran was the first country to recognize it as an independent state in 1991. Although the authoritarian government of Turkmenistan represses that nation's small Shia community, Iran still feels compelled to work closely with it to prevent a spillover of destabilizing Islamic extremists from Afghanistan.. Turkmenistan, like Iran, has also taken a hardline stance against Sunni extremists.[193]

The two nations work together to stem the flow of illegal drugs from Afghanistan. In 2013, Turkmen police oversaw the largest ever seizure of Afghan opium on their border, an operation that was part of a larger anti-drug campaign to crack down on both the drug trade and domestic drug abuse. The two countries have also focused on large-scale oil and gas projects.

WHAT HAS BEEN IRAN'S ROLE IN SYRIA?

Since the Iranian revolution, Syria and Iran have been strategic allies, despite the conflict between Assad's secular Arab nationalism and Iran's revolutionary Islamic ideology. The nations' ties have been political, not religious. (The Assad family belongs to the Alawite branch of Shi'a Islam—Iran's Supreme Leader Ayatollah Khomeini did not even consider Assad to be a true Muslim.) Syria was the first Arab state to recognize the Islamic Republic in 1979.

Both nations shared an antipathy towards Saddam Hussein, as well as towards Israel and the United States. With a few exceptions, the Syrian government was the odd man out in the Arab world in supporting Iran in the Iran-Iraq war.

Both Iran and Syria supported Hezbollah in its struggles against Israel. The U.S. invasion of Iraq, along with the 2006 failed Israeli invasion into Lebanon, brought the countries closer together. Iran supplied Syria with military equipment and heavily invested in the Syrian economy.

Since the 2011 Syrian internal strife, Iran and its Revolutionary Guards weighed in on the side of Assad, sending advisors, special forces, and frontline troops. While it was Russia's military intervention to prop up Assad that was the turning point in the war with ISIS and Western-supported militias, Iran also gained a multi-layered presence in Syria that included local Shiite militants. Iran's Revolutionary Guard was anxious to institutionalize the pro-Iranian militias it had built up in Syria. The Guard wanted to turn the Syrian militias into semi-state actors akin to how Hezbollah operates in Lebanon. This put Iran's Revolutionary Guard at odds with Russia, which wanted to reinforce Syrian state institutions. Iran's President Rouhani, anxious to improve relations with the West, was amenable to disbanding the militias.

It is still unclear how peace will come to war-torn Syria, and what role Iran will play in that process. As of early 2018, however, Syria's future was being decided by Russia, Turkey, and Iran.

WHAT IS IRAN'S RELATIONSHIP WITH THE VARIOUS NON-STATE MILITANTS GROUPS IN THE MIDDLE EAST?

Since the 1979 revolution and its eight-year war with Iraq in the 1980s, Iran has been looking for ways to both protect itself and spread its influence. Using the special forces arm of the Revolutionary Guard—the Quds Force—Iran has sought alliances with non-state actors to pursue its foreign policy objectives. The United States designates some of these non-state actors, such as Hezbollah in Lebanon, as terrorist organizations.

The U.S. cites Iran's links to these groups as the main reason for putting Iran on its list of state sponsors of terrorism. According to the 2016 State Department *Country Reports on Terrorism*, Iran is the foremost state sponsor of terrorism in the world. The report accused Iran of backing anti-Israeli groups, as well as supporting proxies that have destabilized Iraq, Syria, and Yemen. It also accused Iran of supplying weapons, money, and training to militant Shia groups in Bahrain, maintaining cyber terrorism programs, and refusing to prosecute senior members of Al Qaeda that it had detained.[194]

But, as the saying goes, one person's terrorist is another person's freedom fighter. It all depends on where you sit. For many people in the Middle East, Israel is a nation that illegally occupies Palestine and brutally represses the Palestinian people. They see Hezbollah in Lebanon and Hamas in Gaza as legitimate resistance fighters against enemies who are infinitely better armed and have more sophisticated means of killing.

HEZBOLLAH

Iran's most successful non-state relationship is with Hezbollah, whose name is Arabic for Party of God. Starting in the late 1970s, Lebanon's Shia community was ripe with resentment. Despite being the largest sect within Lebanon, the Shia had been left out of much of the decision making in the religious-based political system put in place by the French at a time when Sunnis and Christians made up a larger percentage of the population. Shia strongholds in the south and in parts of Beirut also became home to thousands of Palestinian refugees. Cross border skirmishes with Israel became common.

In 1982, Israel invaded south Lebanon to attack Palestinian militants. Shia leaders, looking for a way to resist the Israeli occupation, challenged the mainstream Shia Amal movement and formed an armed movement that would later become Hezbollah. Early on, they sought support from Iran, and their targets were the Israelis and their American backers.

The United States blamed Hezbollah and Iran for the bombings of the U.S. Embassy and U.S. Marine barracks in Lebanon in 1983. The Marine barracks attack left 258 Americans servicemen dead; at the embassy, the death toll was 63, including 17 Americans. Another bombing at the US Embassy in 1984 left 24 dead.

Hezbollah, which was officially formed in 1985 after years of mobilization, denied any involvement, and a previously unknown group called "Islamic Jihad" took credit for the bombings. Caspar Weinberger, the U.S. Defense Secretary at the time, insisted that U.S. officials never discovered who was responsible.

Hezbollah continued its guerrilla war against Israeli forces in South Lebanon, but also began to play an active role in Lebanese politics. While the U.S. press portrays Hezbollah as an Iranian agent, for Lebanese it is one of the most popular political parties in the country, where it routinely wins among the highest number of votes in the parliament, and where it is widely viewed as a legitimate political party, with an armed wing that succeeded in liberating and defending the country from Israel twice: in 1982 and in 2006.

Iran has used its ties to Hezbollah not just to keep Israel out of Lebanon but also to expand Iran's reach in the region. For Iran, a Shia, Farsi-speaking country in a Sunni-dominated, Arabic-speaking region, Hezbollah not only added military strength but also provided Arabic-speaking cadre who could maneuver more easily in the Arab world. After the U.S. invasion of Iraq in 2003, Iran called on Hezbollah to help train Shiite militias in Iraq to fight U.S. forces. These militias also became involved in sectarian violence, both on their own and in support of the U.S.-installed Shia-dominated government's repression against Sunnis.

In Syria, as the uprising against Bashar al-Assad threatened to topple his regime, Iran intervened to support Assad. When Syrian rebels led by the Nusra Front took control of territory along the Syrian-Lebanese border, Hezbollah joined the fight. Along with the Lebanese Army, they fought a three-year battle to uproot the rebels, including ISIS forces, and succeeded in dislodging ISIS from the border area in August 2017.

Both Hezbollah and Iran emerged as winners in the battle to save Assad and defeat ISIS. But Hezbollah's growing strength contributed to a rise in regional tension, alarming Israel, the United States, and Saudi Arabia. The Saudis were also angry about Hezbollah's condemnation of the U.S.-Saudi bombing of Yemen.

That's why in November 2017, the Saudi Crown Prince concocted a bizarre plan to get at Iran and Hezbollah. He brought the Lebanese Prime Minister Saad Hariri, long backed by Saudi Arabia, to the Saudi capital and pressured him to resign—ostensibly because of the presence of Hezbollah in the Lebanese government. The plan backfired. Returning home, Hariri rescinded his resignation, and the Saudi misadventure only brought more support for Hezbollah, indirectly benefitting Iran.

HAMAS

Iran has also built alliances with Palestinian militia, most notably Hamas, the Palestinian Islamic Jihad, and the Popular Front for the Liberation of Palestine—General Command. The longest relationship is with Islamic Jihad, but the deepest ties have tended to be with Hamas. After the Islamic Revolution, Iran supported the Palestinian cause rhetorically but was not very active. After the Oslo Peace Accords in 1993, which Iran opposed, the Iranians began supporting Hamas and other Palestinian groups that also opposed the U.S.-backed peace process.[195]

With Iran's support of Assad, however, tensions between these Palestinian militias and Iran increased, as some Palestinians— including Hamas—became concerned about the treatment of Palestinian refugees in Syria and spoke out against Assad. In 2012, Hamas broke with Iran. Hamas had never been completely dependent on or a proxy for Iran, but the break meant that Hamas had to forgo much of the funding they had been receiving from Iran, and instead turned to Qatar and Turkey. Since the summer of 2017, there has been somewhat of a reconciliation with Iran.[196]

HOUTHIS IN YEMEN

There is a common misconception that the Houthi rebellion in Yemen is part of a larger Iranian proxy war against Saudi Arabia. The Houthi rebellion grew out of internal political dynamics in Yemen, not Iranian agitation.[197] The Houthis, officially called Ansar Allah, are a homegrown movement that originated in north-ern Yemen in the 1990s and fought against Yemen's government from 2004 to 2010.

In 2014, charging that the government had failed to provide for the needs of the people in northern Yemen, the Houthis rose up against the central government. Some reports insist that Iran was providing weapons, money, and training to the Houthis before they even entered the capital Sana'a in 2014. Others claim that the

Iranians were not involved early on and that they had actually advised the Houthis not to take over the capital.

After the Saudi-led bombing campaign started in March 2015, however, Iran helped the Houthis with training, mostly through Hezbollah (although the Houthis were already experienced fighters from their past wars with the Yemeni central government). Weapons shipments to the Houthis have been reduced by the Saudi's sea blockade, but Iran has reportedly shipped weapons via Somalia, then transferred them to small fishing boats, which are hard to spot because they are so common. Most of the weapons used by the Houthis, however, had been taken from government armories—mostly, weapons the United States had sold to Yemen.

While there are no ideological or strategic imperatives tying Iran and the Houthis, support for the Houthis helps Iran keep the Saudis bogged down in a costly, protracted quagmire that has brought them international condemnation because of the bombing of civilians and civilian infrastructure that has devastated Yemen.

WHAT IS IRAN'S RELATIONSHIP WITH RUSSIA?

Iran and Russia have a long history. Dating back to the Safavid period in Iran, historians can point to various interactions between Persians and Russians. The relationship has often been filled with suspicion and tension due to Russia's historical interference in Iran's internal affairs.

More recently, Russia and Iran have come together due to shared interests. First, Syria has strategic importance for the two nations, and both were anxious to make sure Assad was not overthrown. Additionally, both wanted to push back against Sunni extremism globally. Since the time of the Soviet-Afghan war in the 1980s, Tehran and Moscow have had a shared animosity towards

Sunni Islamist groups and have been wary of the links some Western powers had forged with these groups.

A second factor for closer ties has been the isolation both countries have faced from the West. Iran has been isolated due to its nuclear program and its links with groups like Hezbollah. Russia's actions in Ukraine and Crimea have left it facing sanctions from the West.

Russia played a key role in negotiating the Iran nuclear deal, and after the accord was signed, its relationship with Iran became stronger. Iran had already relied heavily on Russian weapons to supply its military, but those ties deepened as Russia removed its own restrictions on selling more sophisticated weapons to Iran.

Additionally, the countries have extensive trade links. In 2017 alone, they signed energy agreements worth $30 billion. These range from the development of Iran's oil and gas fields to collaboration on research. They have moved beyond trade in fossil fuels into telecoms and agriculture, and they plan to expand multilateral cooperation in Central Asia and the Caucasus.

On the negative side, Russia has developed a military connection with Israel that concerns Iran, and Russia has increased its ties to some of Iran's Arab adversaries, including Saudi Arabia.[198]

Friction has also developed around Syria. While Russia and Iran worked together in their military campaigns to support Assad, in negotiating Syria's future, Iran felt that Russia had negotiated with the United States and others behind its back.

WHAT RELATIONSHIP DOES IRAN HAVE WITH THE ASIAN POWERS? CHINA? INDIA? JAPAN? SOUTH KOREA? AUSTRALIA?

When it comes to regional powers in the east, many of Iran's relationships are centered around oil. China, India, Japan, Korea, and even Australia require oil and its derivatives to fuel their economic growth—and Iran has the oil.

China's interest, however, goes even further. China is seeking to check American power in the Middle East, just as they are in every other region. They see Iran as a lynchpin for their objectives. China is seeking Iranian partnership in implementing its Silk Road Economic Belt initiative, and is trying to build a transportation network that connects China to Europe, bypassing the Red Sea and Mediterranean.[199]

For Iran, China provides a market for its energy resources, and receives critical investment and help modernizing its oil and natural gas sector. Ironically, the Chinese foothold in Iran came about because Western sanctions on Iran kept Western firms out of Iranian markets.[200]

Additionally, Iran and China have slowly built a solid military relationship, including weapons sales, training, and joint naval exercises in the Persian Gulf.[201] This relationship could prove far more advantageous to Iran than its military relationship with Russia, mainly because the Chinese do not have military ties to Iran's adversaries in the Middle East.

Japan and South Korea's alliance with the U.S. makes their relationships with Iran much more problematic. Like China, these countries need access to oil, but they also rely on the U.S. security umbrella. Deeper ties beyond the energy sector would cause tension with the United States.[202] Additionally, Iran's closeness with China makes both Japan and South Korea nervous. With the removal of some sanctions after the signing of the nuclear deal, however, both nations have upped their investments in Iran.[203]

Australia's relations have taken a different path. While access to energy is important, Australia has made its relationship with the U.S. paramount. Trade with Iran has been minimal, especially after Australia imposed its own set of sanctions in 2008. Australia does see some common interests, viewing Iran as a partner in fighting ISIS and creating a stable Iraq. But on balance, the relationship remains limited at best.[204]

India, like China, is a significant importer of Iranian crude oil. Sanctions have slowed trade between both countries, but recently the Indians have stepped up investment inside Iran, including funding for the new port of Chabahar. India wants to develop the north-south corridor that connects Central Asia to the Persian Gulf. Closer ties between India and Iran have caused tension with Pakistan.[205]

WHAT RELATIONSHIP DOES IRAN HAVE WITH LATIN AMERICA AND AFRICA?

Latin America and Africa often get overlooked when discussing Iran's relations across the globe. While not nearly as influential or extensive as the U.S. or China, Iran nonetheless has established a foothold on both continents. Iran's aims are centered around three main factors: easing its Western-imposed isolation due to sanctions, countering U.S.-Israeli-Saudi influence, and creating strategic depth in case Iran is attacked.

In Africa, Iran has engaged Shia communities in various African countries to challenge Saudi Arabia's Sunni influence. It has set up schools and brings thousands of students from across Africa to study in Iran's religious center, Qom. It has also helped fund Shia social welfare centers, with soup kitchens and homeless shelters. Saudi diplomatic cables released in 2015 by WikiLeaks reveal Saudi concern about Iran's Shiite expansion in Mali, Mauritania, Burkina Faso, and Nigeria in West Africa.[206] The funds and the outreach, however, pale in comparison to the billions of dollars and the thousands of schools and mosques set up by the Saudis.

In terms of allies at the national level in Africa, Sudan was once a solid Iranian ally. The Sudanese relationship was built on a mutual distrust of the Western-dominated international system. Despite representing different sects of Islam, the two countries developed a robust military relationship. Iran had even used Sudan as a land route to smuggle weapons to Hamas. But in 2016, the Sudanese severed ties with Iran due to pressure from Saudi Arabia, which financed Sudan after its loss of revenue when oil-rich South Sudan gained independence in 2011.[207]

Sudan's neighbor, Eritrea, is another of Iran's curious alliances, given that it is a country of Christians and Sunni Muslims. As the Eritreans emerged from a long conflict to gain independence from Ethiopia in 1991, many Eritreans hoped their nation would come into the Western orbit. But continued U.S. support for Ethiopia forced Eritrea to look elsewhere. Iran saw Eritrea's disgruntlement as an opportunity to gain a foothold in the Red Sea. It wanted to use Eritrea as a waystation for funneling weapons to the Houthis in Yemen, as well as to Hamas in Gaza. Iran's operations in Eritrea are part of its larger goal of controlling the Bab el Mandeb strait and the water route to the Suez Canal. Also, the United States and France have large bases in neighboring Djibouti, so a presence in Eritrea could help Iran with intelligence gathering.

Oddly enough, Israel also operates in Eritrea, maintaining a listening facility to monitor Iranian activities in the Red Sea.[208] Cooperating with Israel was a way for the Eritrean government to balance its controversial relationship with Iran. Even odder was the revelation in a 2016 report by the UN Monitoring Group on Somalia and Eritrea that Eritrea had sent 400 soldiers to fight alongside the Saudis in Yemen against the Houthis, who are supported by Iran; Eritrea denied the report.[209]

Iran's relations with other African countries may cause some anxiety in the West and with the Saudis, but their activities have been minimal, and their African hosts seem to easily switch sides when a better deal is offered.[210]

LATIN AMERICA

Heading west to Latin America, we see similar trends. Iran has formed ties with leaders searching for ways to buck the U.S.-led international order. Iran's most important partner in Latin America has been Venezuela. Since 1999, when the revolutionary leader Hugo Chavez came to power, the relationship experienced a rapid expansion. Both countries saw themselves as the vanguard against U.S. interference in the region, and both have been the victims of US sanctions. Their relationship has mainly focused on oil, manufacturing, and trade partnerships.

Iran built close relations with Bolivia when Evo Morales became president in 2006. As in Venezuela, the relationship was built on opposition to the U.S.-led global order. Cuba, Ecuador, and Nicaragua also developed closer links along the same lines.

Another partner in the region has been Brazil, due to trade in the energy sector. In 2010, the Brazilians, along with Turkey, attempted to find a solution to the nuclear impasse with Iran. While they were able to get an agreement from Iran, the United States and other international players refused to honor their attempts.

Iran has been seeking relationships in Africa and Latin America in hopes of curtailing its sanctions-imposed isolation. After signing the nuclear deal, Iran's need for immediate and sizable investment meant it would lean more heavily on Russia and China, leaving out smaller and poorer countries in Africa and Latin America. Also, increased trade and cooperation with the U.S. by some potential partners has meant Iran faces a dwindling number of choices. Most countries are unwilling to give up lucrative trade with the powerful United States in exchange for comparatively paltry deals with Iran.

*****

While Iran is a mid-level power battered by decades of sanctions, it is still remarkable to see how the government of Iran has leveraged its meager resources and ideological fervor to have a major influence abroad. Many Iranians, however, would much prefer that their government focus on improving the lives of its citizens and building beneficial trade relations instead of spreading its theology and military zeal beyond its borders.

CHAPTER 10: THE WAY FORWARD

As I conclude this book in early 2018, Iran has just emerged from a period of internal turmoil. A series of protests that began on December 28, 2017 and lasted for several weeks shook the nation. The protests, which began over economic hardships suffered by the young and working class, quickly spread to more than 80 cities and towns, making them the largest public manifestation of discontent in Iran since the disputed 2009 presidential election.

The protests reflected the unfulfilled expectations of Iran's working class and young people. President Rouhani had won re-election in 2017 by promising more jobs for Iran's youth through more foreign investment, as well as more social justice, individual freedom, and political tolerance. The economic promises rested on the notion that Rouhani would be able to deliver a nuclear deal that would lift sanctions and revive the economy. Rouhani delivered on the nuclear deal, but the infusion of funds that came with the partial lifting of sanctions did not improve the lives of ordinary Iranians.

To make matters worse, in December 2017, the government undertook a number of economic austerity measures that led to a hike in fuel prices and other basic goods. An epidemic of avian influenza killed 15 million chickens, further inflating the price for eggs and chicken, the most popular and affordable foods for Iranians.

That same month, Iranian President Hassan Rouhani had proposed a new budget and made it open for the public to see. Many were angry when they discovered that it called for slashing

MEDEA BENJAMIN

subsidies for the poor while allocating enormous funds for Iran's wealthy religious foundations, some of which were linked to corrupt credit institutions that had depleted the savings of many Iranians. Some people were also upset to see such a large chuck of the budget going to the powerful military and paramilitary forces, including $8 billion for the Revolutionary Guards.

The protests that broke out in December 2017 initially focused on high prices and corruption. But they soon took on a rare political dimension, rejecting the entire system and denouncing Supreme Leader Ayatollah Khamenei, President Rouhani, and the Revolutionary Guards. Some of the protesters also condemned Iran's overseas interventions, calling for the nation's resources to be spent at home.

Many speculated that conservative opponents of moderate President Rouhani had started the demonstrations as a way to capitalize on public frustration but that they quickly lost control of both the message and the actions.

While most protesters were peaceful, some became violent, attacking shops, cars, government buildings, and even police stations. The government called in the police and Revolutionary Guards to quash the demonstrations. Twenty-two people were killed in clashes and more than 1,000 were arrested. The government also countered the protests by organizing large pro-government rallies.

The Revolutionary Guard blamed the unrest on the United States, Israel, and Saudi Arabia, as well as the exiled opposition group MEK (the People's Mujahadeen of Iran) and supporters of the monarchy that had been overthrown in the 1979 revolution.

President Rouhani was more sympathetic. He said that despite the exploitation of the protests by outsiders, the demonstrators had legitimate economic, political, and social grievances. He also pointed out the generational element to the unrest, saying, "We cannot pick a lifestyle and tell two generations after us to live like that. It is impossible... The views of the young generation about life and the world is different than ours." Over 90 percent of the people arrested during the protests were under age 25.

To the dismay of the Trump administration and other anti-regime forces, the protests fizzled out after a few weeks. Their demise was due to the government crackdown, but also because they had no central leadership, did not put forth coherent demands, failed to get widespread support, and posed no realistic alternative to the regime. But they did strike a chord, revealing a level of anger and frustration that will remain until the government takes concrete steps to address their economic grievances.

It will be difficult to significantly improve the economy, however, as long as the fate of nuclear deal and sanctions hang in the balance. When the nuclear agreement was signed in 2015, many Iranians rejoiced over the chance to "rejoin the world" because the deal was not just about nukes. It was also about the future direction of Iran. Just as American conservatives tried to scuttle the deal, so did conservatives in Iran. They wanted Iran to stand up to the West, not negotiate. They were afraid that Western influence would pollute the revolution—and diminish their power. They feared that President Rouhani would end up like President Mikhail Gorbachev, whose reforms and detente with the West led to the unraveling of the Soviet Union.

The nuclear deal marked a triumph over the hardliners in both countries. A milestone for diplomacy, it was a tectonic shift from the past, when officials from Iran and the United States were not even authorized to speak to one another. In the course of the intense negotiations, American and Iranian diplomats became acquainted—some would even say they became friends. Republicans in Washington chided Secretary of State John Kerry for what they considered his "chummy relationship" with Iran's American-educated Foreign Minister Mohammad Javad Zarif.

The triumphant negotiations led many to believe that the nuclear deal would pave the way for talks on a wide range of other issues, from Iran's development of ballistic missiles to the conflicts in Afghanistan, Iran, Syria, and Yemen. Coordination on these critical areas could have helped to bring an end to those long, agonizing conflicts.

Storming into this fragile space like a bull in a China shop came Donald Trump, excoriating the nuclear deal and blaming Iran for all the troubles in the Middle East. He ran over to Saudi Arabia to sell more weapons—and participate in a traditional war dance with the Saudi king. Not only did Trump and King Salman bond, but a "bromance" developed between the next generation: Salman's young, aggressive son and heir to the throne, Mohammed bin Salman, and Trump's son-in-law Jared Kushner.

President Trump managed to infuriate Iranians of all political stripes when he added Iran to the list of countries whose citizens would be banned from entering the United States, hurting countless Iranian families who had nothing to do with the hostilities.

Another example of Trump's ability to offend all Iranians was when he accused Iran of harassing American ships "in the Arabian Gulf." The Arabian Gulf? Really? Iranians went wild. All Iranians call this body of water that separates them from their Arab neighbors "the Persian Gulf." So do cartographers. President Rouhani ridiculed Trump for his ignorance of geography. "Trump should ask his military what is written as the name of this gulf," he jested. Nearly three million Iranians bombarded Trump's Instagram account with nasty comments.

When protests broke out at the end of Demember 2017, Trump gave his full support, saying "The people of Iran are finally acting against the brutal and corrupt Iranian regime," and ridiculously tried to take the issue to the UN Security Council. The Iranian government condemned what it called "grotesque interference" in the country's domestic affairs, and used this interference to rally internal support for the government. Whether Iranians were pro- or anti-government, the idea that Donald Trump cared about their well-being seemed like a cruel joke.

*****

The American demonization of Iran did not start with Trump. Since 1979, it has run deep and wide in mainstream US politics, among both Democrats and Republicans. Officials in both parties have repeatedly declared themselves ready and eager to "strike" and "obliterate" Iran. Republican Senator John McCain sang, "Bomb, bomb, bomb Iran," to the tune of an old Beach Boys song and embraced the murderous MEK that is so hated by most Iranians.[211] Democratic Congressman Brad Sherman said U.S. sanctions should be strong enough to "hurt the Iranian people."[212] Billionaire political funder Sheldon Adelson called for an unprovoked nuclear attack on Iran.

The U.S. military has been threatening Iran as well. General Joseph Votel, head of the U.S. Central Command, told Congress that the U.S. must be prepared to use military means to confront and defeat the "greatest destabilizing force in the Middle East."[213] Admiral James Lyons Jr., former commander of the U.S. Pacific Fleet, said the U.S. military was prepared to "drill them back to the fourth century."[214]

President Trump took the dregs of this belligerence and turned it into his foreign policy. He brought the most diehard Iran-haters into his cabinet. He surrounded himself with people itching to, in the words of Senator John McCain, "Bomb, bomb, bomb Iran."

*****

To single out Iran as the source of global terrorism is absurd. According to the Global Terrorism Database of King's College

London, more than 94 percent of the deaths caused by Islamic terrorism from 2001 to 2016 were perpetrated by ISIS, Al Qaeda, and other Sunni jihadists. Iran is fighting those groups, not fueling them. Iran is a Shia nation combatting Sunni jihadists who consider Shia, and Westerners, infidels. Not one Iranian has ever been linked to a terrorist attack in the United States.

If Americans want to assign blame for Middle Eastern instability and terrorism, how about starting with the United States? The greatest single action in modern history to destabilize the region was the 2003 U.S. invasion of Iraq. American interventions in the Middle East have ignited civil wars, religious fanaticism, and vicious sectarianism.

Another appropriate place to point the finger is Saudi Arabia. Saudi money and ideology have fueled Sunni jihadists from the time of the mujahedeen in Afghanistan. The Saudis only stopped funding Al Qaeda and ISIS after those groups started biting the hand that fed them. In the West, almost every terrorist attack has had some connection to Saudi Arabia. Why, then, did the Trump administration put Iranians, not Saudis, on the list of people banned from entry to the United States?

"The United States cast off the most populous, cohesive country in the region, Iran, in favor of a bunch of corrupt, venal, terrorist-supporting dudes in Saudi Arabia. It is unconscionable," said Colonel Larry Wilkerson, former chief of staff for Colin Powell, who was Secretary of State under the Bush administration.[215]

Sadly, even tragically, that's not how most Americans see it. Following the narrative propagated by politicians and the mainstream media, Americans rank Iran alongside North Korea as one of their "greatest enemies."[216]

This doesn't make any sense. Iran is not a credible threat to the United States. Its military may be good at confronting ISIS, but it is no match for the U.S. military. Iran spends somewhere between

$15 billon and $30 billion a year on its military while the United States spends $700 billion.[217] U.S. ally Saudi Arabia, with one-third of Iran's population, has far superior weaponry, thanks to U.S. weapons sales. In terms of military spending, Saudi Arabia ranks third in the world, after the behemoths U.S. and China, while Iran ranks number 19.[218] Even Turkey and Egypt, two other major powers in the region, are militarily superior to Iran.

What about Iran's nuclear threat? The inspections regime Iran agreed to under the nuclear deal is the most rigorous inspections regime ever negotiated. And while the world would be a safer place if Iran did not have nuclear weapons, the same can be said of *all* nations. We agonize over Iran's potential to acquire a nuclear bomb while our ally, Israel, has somewhere between 80 and 200 nuclear warheads and, in stark contrast to Iran, has flatly refused to sign the non-proliferation treaty (NPT). The volatile and repressive government of Pakistan, on Iran's border, also has nuclear weapons. And, what about the United States itself? The U.S. is a signatory to the NPT but has defied its treaty obligations by spending outrageous sums of money to upgrade its nuclear arsenal and by failing to make real progress in nuclear disarmament.

Iran is a powerful nation, but it will never be a superpower. Iran tries to increase its influence by spreading Shi'ism, but this brand of Islam represents only about 10–15 percent of Muslims worldwide. The overwhelming majority of Muslims are Sunni. So even in a religious war, Iran could never win.

While the U.S. accuses Iran of pursuing regional hegemony, ironically, Iran's regional strength has come mainly from the American overthrow of the Taliban in Afghanistan and Saddam Hussein in Iraq. Contrary to U.S. propaganda, Iran's aim is not to take over in the Middle East but to preserve itself. Given the lingering trauma of the war with Iraq, the Saudi-Sunni rivalry, and the hostility of the U.S. superpower, Tehran's primary objective is defense and survival. It wants friendly and stable governments on its borders. Unlike more distant powers, Iran has permanent interests in neighboring Iraq, Syria, and Afghanistan and is affected when there is conflict in neighboring countries. Iran wants to ensure that it will not be attacked by unfriendly nations, whether Israel, the United States, Saudi Arabia, or an aggressive neighbor (such as the attack by Iraq in 1980). It also wants to protect itself from terrorist activities at home.

The U.S. military concurs. According to the U.S. Defense Department, "Iran's military doctrine is defense. It is designed to deter an attack, survive an initial strike, retaliate against an aggressor, and force a diplomatic solution to hostilities while avoiding any concessions that challenge its core interests."[219]

*****

If Iran is no threat to the United States, then why is the U.S. government so hostile towards Iran? The answer is that U.S. policy in the Middle East has been hijacked by a variety of actors who are out for their own interests.

For starters, there is the long-standing U.S. relationship with the Saudi monarchy, which is obsessed with its rival Iran. The United States should not be taking sides in this regional feud. In an April 2016 interview in *The Atlantic*, President Obama expressed his frustration with the destabilizing Saudi-Iranian rivalry. "The competition between the Saudis and the Iranians—which has helped to feed proxy wars and chaos in Syria and Iraq and Yemen—requires us to say to our friends [the Saudis] as well as to the Iranians that they need to find an effective way to share the neighborhood and institute some sort of cold peace," Obama said.[220] Instead of encouraging the Saudis, the U.S. should be pushing them to "share the neighborhood."

U.S. policy has also been hijacked by the Israeli government, especially under Prime Minister Benjamin Netanyahu. For

Netanyahu, Iran acts as a foil to divert attention from his own oppressive policies toward Palestinians in the West Bank, Gaza, and East Jerusalem. Obama was willing to defy Netanyahu's opposition to the Iran deal, but Trump swallowed the Netanyahu position—hook, line, and sinker. When Trump decertified the Iran deal, Netanyahu was elated, calling it "a very brave decision that is right for the world."

The leaders of Israel and Saudi Arabia have been so eager to shape a more aggressive U.S. policy toward Iran that they downplayed their animosity towards each other and began collaborating. Former Secretary of State John Kerry said that leaders of both nations pressured Obama to bomb Iran instead of signing a deal. "Each of them said to me, you have to bomb Iran, it's the only thing they are going to understand," Kerry said.[221] Tragically, what this really suggests is that threats and bombing are the only things that the present leaders of Israel and Saudi Arabia understand.

U.S. policy towards Iran has also been hijacked by weapons makers and Pentagon contractors whose very lucrative livelihoods (and shareholder benefits) are tied to peddling fear and justifying a constant state of war. For these "merchants of death," as Pope Francis calls them, Iran is a gold mine. They rake in enormous profits from U.S. military assistance and weapons sales to anti-Iran countries such as Israel, Saudi Arabia, the Emirates and Bahrain. They also make a fortune from what American taxpayers spend to keep about 30,000 U.S. troops, ships, and aircraft in the Gulf (somewhere between $50 billion and $90 billion a year).

Finally, others who influence U.S. policy towards Iran are the bottom feeders who suck up the crumbs—the American politicians who receive donations from pro-Israel groups, the lobbyists in the pay of the weapons industries and foreign governments, the pundits whose "think tanks" are bankrolled by Lockheed Martin or some Saudi prince, and national-security bureaucrats whose careers and bank accounts are enhanced by the constant threat of war.

WHERE WILL CHANGE COME FROM?

Iranians needs to get out from under the yoke of both internal hardliners and international pressure so that they can transform the nation into a more open and democratic society.

Some say the only way this transformation will happen is by overthrowing the present regime. They point to the election of three presidents claiming to be reformists—Akbar Hashemi Rafsanjani, Mohammad Khatami, and Hassan Rouhani. All three were unable to implement most of their promised reforms. They also point to the crushing of the nonviolent, reformist Green Movement and the more recent quashing of the January 2018 wave of protests.

But is violent revolution an option? Who could overthrow the regime? The National Council of Resistance in Iran, which is really the same as the People's Mujahedeen of Iran (MEK), puts itself forward as a group with cadre inside Iran, ready to take over. But this group has almost zero support inside Iran.

What about separatist minority groups rising up to overthrow the regime? Together, these minority groups make up quite a large portion of the population—about 40 percent. For many years, the United States covertly supported separatist groups inside Iran to destabilize the country. Of the minorities, the Kurds have historically been the group pressing the hardest for greater autonomy or separation. The militant Kurdish separatists were defeated in the 1980s, although the CIA, together with Israel's Mossad, continued to provide covert support during the Bush years and, according to the Iranian government, the Obama years as well. There are also separatists among the Baluchis in southeastern Iran, Arabs in the southwest, and some Azeri Turks in the northwest. But these minorities have been part of Iran for ages, and most are well integrated. The Azeris, Iran's largest minority, are the most fully integrated. The Supreme Leader Ayatollah Ali Khamenei is Azeri. Efforts over the years to encourage uprisings by these various ethnic groups have come to naught. Meanwhile, the regime's coercive apparatus has only become more heavily armed, more organized, and more battle-hardened.

How about more sanctions? Could even tighter sanctions cause the regime to crumble? This strategy hasn't worked since 1979—and has even less chance of working now. Since the signing of the nuclear deal, the rest of the world is moving ahead with all kinds of business ventures. The White House would face a major international backlash if it unilaterally reinstated nuclear-related sanctions, including secondary sanctions on foreign firms doing business with Iran.

Looking at the recent history of the Middle East, a more important question to ask is: Even if the regime could be overthrown, what would follow? Another failed state like Iraq, Afghanistan, Libya, and Syria? The track record for regime change in the region is dismal.

CHANGE FROM WITHIN

A nonviolent process of transformation from within is really the only option. Fortunately, demographics are on the side of change.

The sector holding back change is primarily the older, religious generation, and that generation is, literally, dying out. Supreme Leader Ali Khamenei is elderly and in poor health; so are many of the clerics and politicians from the days of the revolution.

MEDEA BENJAMIN

Most Iranians were born after 1979; two-thirds of the population is under 25. The nation's restless youth, particularly those living in urban areas, want more economic options and social freedom.

The government tries to control the population in ways that range from operations by the secret police to vetting candidates for election to pervasive propaganda, but Iranians are well educated and generally well informed. While the state controls television broadcasting, and satellite dishes are technically illegal, some 70 percent of Iranians own satellite receivers and have access to programs from all over the world. The government blocks some websites like Facebook and Reddit, but Iranians easily find ways around the blocks or use encrypted messaging apps like Telegram. There are about 75,000 bloggers; the Internet is abuzz with critiques and ideas. Out of 80 million people, 48 million Iranians have smartphones and 40 million use Telegram messenger.

Iranians are also not physically isolated. Many travel to Europe or the United States on vacation or to study. There are about 50,000 Iranians studying around the world, some 9,000 of them in the United States.

About five million Iranians live abroad, mostly in North America, Europe, Australia, and the greater Middle East. This number keeps growing every year, as some 160,000 Iranians emigrate in search of better economic opportunities. Many of them maintain regular contact with their family and friends in Iran. With constant travel in and out of the country, Iranians understand the pros and cons of other societies, and this information informs and elevates their push for change back home.

*****

Looking at the history of Iran in the last century alone, we see that Iranians have a remarkable record of political activism. In more recent history, since the 1979 upheaval, Iranians have been putting their lives at risk to organize human rights groups, women's organizations, unions, legal collectives, and other forms of social activism. They have come out on the streets to protest. Iranian prisoners of conscience have gone on prolonged hunger strikes to call attention to their plight. Activists have staged hunger strikes outside prisons to protest the mistreatment of prisoners and the lack of due process. Women regularly defy the government-imposed dress code. Student groups protest the rising costs of higher education, the privatization of student services, gender and religious discrimination, and the presence of security forces on campuses.

Many activists end up in prison. Others escape and seek refuge abroad. Most, however, remain in Iran and continue their courageous work. They have had success in opening up opportunities for women, invigorating the electoral system, loosening the dress code, creating more government transparency, fighting corruption, making the judicial system more accountable, decreasing the use of the death penalty, and pushing for economic subsidies for the poor. For many, however, the reforms have been painfully slow and as the December 2017 protests showed, there is little articulaton between the organized activst groups and the unorganized, pent-up frustration of Iranian youth.

The best way that we, as outsiders, can help speed up the process of reform is to stop our governments from threatening Iran, imposing more sanctions, destroying the nuclear deal, or actually waging war. When international tensions ease, Iranians have more breathing room. Our job is to get our governments out of the way so that the Iranian people can, as they have done so brilliantly in their past, transform their own nation.

*****

On the last day of my visit to Iran in 2014, I spent some time shopping for gifts to take home. In one of the lovely craft stores, I fell into a conversation with the owner. He was delighted that I was from the United States, and had lots of questions: What did I think of Barack Obama? Did I like Iranian food? Did I know his cousin in Los Angeles? We chatted for a while, and then I left without buying anything.

The storekeeper ran after me, holding a beautiful painting in his hand. "I want to give you this," he said. "It was painted by a friend of mine." He handed me a painting of a large, traditional family sitting on the floor in front of a low table brimming with food—kebabs, rice, beef kofte, flatbread, pomegranates. "When you go home, I want you to think of the people of our two nations sitting around a table together, eating good food, enjoying good conversation, meeting each other's families. That is how it should be."

I tearfully accepted the glorious gift. Once home, I put it in a gold frame and hung it on the wall in the entryway to our house. I look at it as I go in and out of the house every day. It serves as a reminder of the generosity of the Iranian people and the way things might one day evolve between our nations.

Prime Minister Mossadegh and President Truman, 1951. Mossadegh was overthrown in a CIA coup in 1953.
Photo credit: Abbie Rowe.

Man in US with sign during Iran hostage crisis, 1979.
Photo credit: Marion S. Trikosko.

Coronation of Reza Shah, 1926.

Morality police (woman in chador) chastising a young Iranian for wearing an "improper" hijab.

Young Iranian man and woman socializing at a cafe in Tehran, 2015.
Photo credit: Medea Benjamin.

Author (third from right) visits woman-owned medical supplies business, 2015.
Photo credit: Medea Benjamin.

Protesting voter fraud during the Green Movement in 2011.
Getty Images.

Secretary of State John Kerry and Foreign Minister Javad Zarif during
Iran Nuclear Deal talks.
Photo credit: Dominick Reuter/AFP/Getty Images.

Iranian President Hassan Rouhani, elected in 2013 and re-elected in
2017.

Isfahan Mosque highlights Iran's beautiful 5,000 year old culture.

Women elected to the Iranian National Assembly in 2017.
Photo credit: Shahrvand.

Statue of Shah being torn down during 1979 Revolution.

Zoroastrian temple in Yazd.
Photo credit: Zenith210.

Vank Cathedral, Armenian Quarter, Isfahan, Iran.
Photo credit: Mike Gadd.

Young Iranian Kurds.
Photo credit: Abdul Hamid Zibari.

ACKNOWLEDGEMENTS

Hats off to Sandy Davies for his invaluable work on the history of Iran that became the basis for chapters one and two, and to David Shams for his rigorous help on the very complicated chapters about Iran's relations with the U.S., the Middle East, and beyond. David's personal understanding of Iran helped me navigate some treacherous political waters.

A big thanks to Brienne Kordis for being such a terrific assistant and great researcher and editor. I give my deepest appreciation to Leila Zand for her deep insights into her beautiful culture and country, from taking us there to giving critical feedback on the book. Crystal Zevon gave me marvelous editing help, as did the very knowledgeable Ann Wright. Thanks to Marin Kirk for your research and Elliot Swain for being a critical reader, and helping to gather the photos. I so appreciate Phyllis Bennis and Vijay Prashad for helping me sort out some of the thorny political points concerning Iran's regional allies.

My ever encouraging and upbeat publisher John Oakes and the entire OR team are a delight to work with.

My life partner, Tighe Barry, has been sweetly tolerant of my late night writing and constantly supportive—from hot tea to shoulder rubs. Thanks to my daughters, Maya and Arlen, and their families, for their shared concerns and efforts to make the world a more peaceful place.

I am ever indebted to CODEPINK cofounder Jodie Evans, with whom I have had the great honor and privilege of working with for the past 16 years, sharing our grief at the violence that surrounds us and optimism that citizen activism can lead the way to a more loving planet. I so appreciate the CODEPINK family that I get to work so closely with, including Farida Sharalam, Ariel Gold, Taylor Morley, Nancy Mancias, Mark Folkman, Mariana Mendoza, and Haley Pedersen. Paki Wieland, our "house mom" in D.C., makes the CODEPINK house glow with warmth even on the coldest days.

I am indebted to the work of the National Iranian American Council (NIAC), especially Trita Parsi. I so appreciate Trita's analysis and dedication to stop the U.S. and Iran from going to war. I also thank Marjan Shallal for helping me understand and fall in love with Iranian culture.

Finally, I send my thanks to the many people I have met on trips to Iran who fill me with hope and inspire me to bring our nations closer together.

FURTHER RESOURCES

A History of Iran: Empire of the Mind
Michael Axworthy
Renowned Arab and Islamic Studies professor Michael Axworthy writes eloquently and authoritatively about Iran's fascinating and complex history, taking us through each era from the early Zoroastrians to the challenges of modern-day Iran.

A History of Modern Iran
Ervand Abrahamian
As Abrahamian trances Iran's traumatic journey through the twentieth century, he adroitly negotiates the twists and turns of the country's regional and international politics--always keeping the people of Iran at the center of the narrative.

Losing an Enemy: Obama, Iran, and the Triumph of Diplomacy
Trita Parsi
This book focuses on President Obama's strategy toward Iran's nuclear program and reveals how the historic agreement of 2015 broke the persistent stalemate in negotiations that had blocked earlier efforts.

Bitter Friends, Bosom Enemies: Iran, the U.S., and the Twisted Path to Confrontation
Barbara Slavin

Slavin reveals that relations between Washington and Tehran have been riddled with contradictions for decades and details missed opportunities for reconciliation.

Iran Without Borders
Hamid Dabashi
Acclaimed cultural critic and scholar of Iranian history traces the evolution of this worldly culture from the eighteenth century to the present day.

Close Up
Hamid Dabashi
Dabashi dissects the idea of the oriental in western perceptions of Iranian cinema and details the way that film festivals and distribution in the west have shaped domestic output in Iran.

Operation Ajax
Mike de Seve
This is the story of the CIA coup that removed the democratically elected Mossadegh and reinstated the monarchy.

In the Rose Garden of the Martyrs
Christopher de Bellaigue
An insider's account of Iran and its people, it glides easily between memoir and history of the Islamic revolution and the terrible legacy of the Iran-Iraq war.

All the Shah's Men: An American Coup and the Roots of Middle East Terror
Stephen Kinzer
Kinzer's account of the CIA-orchestrated coup in 1953 makes vital reading for anyone interested in the roots of the revolution.

The Ayatollah Begs to Differ: the Paradox of Modern Iran
Hooman Majd
The grandson of an ayatollah and the son of an Iranian diplomat, Hooman Majd offers a unique perspective on Iran's complex culture.

The Last Great Revolution: Turmoil and Transformation in Iran
Robin B. Wright
A rich history of the events of the 1979 Islamic revolution and its aftermath, including wide-ranging interviews with a variety of Iranians.

Lipstick Jihad
Azadeh Moaveni
A young reporter who grew up in California returns to her parents' homeland in this insightful memoir with illuminating anecdotes.

The Essential Rumi
Jalal al-Din Rumi
Rumi, the 13th century Persian poet, is widely acknowledged as being the greatest Sufi mystic of his age. He was the founder of the brotherhood of the Whirling Dervishes. This is a collection of his exquisite poetry.

Poems from the Divan of Hafiz
Gertrude Bell, translator
Khwaja Shemsundin Mahommad Hifiz-e Sirazi, or simply Hafiz, was a14th century mystical poet of Shiraz. His collected works (The Divan) represent a masterpiece of Persian poetry and are to be found in the homes of many Iranians, who learn his poems by heart and still use them as proverbs and sayings.

Modern Iran: Roots and Results of Revolution
Nikki R Keddie
Updated version of the classic work includes a probing and percep-
tive guide to more than two decades of tumultuous development-
ments, including Iran's nuclear policy and US relations.

Iran Awakening: A Memoir of Revolution and Hope
Shirin Ibadi
Shirin Ebadi won the 2003 Nobel Peace Prize for her work advocating for oppressed peoples. *Iran Awakening* is Ebadi's memoir in
which she describes her upbringing in pre-Revolutionary Iran, as
well as the ways in which the Revolution changed her marriage,
her faith, and her career. It is a powerful condemnation of the
Islamic regime.

Days of God: The Revolution in Iran and its Consequences
James Buchan
Persian scholar and a former foreign correspondent writes an
in-depth account of the revolutionary birth of theocracy in Iran,
using declassified diplomatic papers and Persian-language news
report and interviews.

Shah of Shahs
Ryszard Kapuscinski
Travel writer and war correspondent Kapuscinski describes the
final years of the Shah with a compelling history of conspiracy,
repression, fanatacism, and revolution.

The Mantle of the Prophet: Religion and Politics in Iran
Roy Mottahedeh
A great read for anyone interested in an in-depth look at Ayatollah Khomeini, the roots of the revolution, and the origins of the Islamic Republic.

Persia through Writers' Eyes
David Blow
A wonderful series of selections from 3,000 years of descriptive writing, including everyone from Herodotus to John Simpson.

The Blindfold Horse: Memories of a Persian Childhood
Shusha Guppy
An enchanting account of growing up in Persia before the revolution in a society balanced between traditional Islamic life and the transforming forces of westernization.

Persepolis, the Story of a Childhood and Persepolis 2, the Story of a Return
Marjan Satrapi
Satrapi uses the form of the graphic novel to describe life in Iran before and after the revolution through her eyes as a child. Magnificent, moving, and highly original.

Children of Paradise: The Struggle for the Soul of Iran
Laura Secor
This deep look inside Iranian society shows that beneath the country's monolithic exterior, there are dreamers and doers who are shaping Iran's future.

My Uncle Napoleon: A Novel
Iraj Pezeshkzad
A hilarious tale of family life in early 1940s Tehran. This satirical novel features an aristocratic Iranian family led by "Dear Uncle Napoleon" who oversees the group with an iron fist. The story is told from the perspective of Dear Uncle's least favorite nephew and reflects the end of the pre-Revolutionary era.

Jasmine and Stars, Reading More Than Lolita in Tehran
Fatemeh Keshavarz
Blending first-hand recollections of her own life in 1960s Shiraz, Keshavarz shows the intellectual complexity of Iran.

My Father's Notebook
Kader Abdolah
Abdolah's autobiographical novel sees Iran's recent history through the eyes of a father and son, unraveling an intricate tale of moving from the silent world of a village carpet-mender to the increasingly hostile environment of modern Iran.

GUIDEBOOKS
Iran, Bradt Travel Guide
Hilary Smith
A great guide to Iran, combining practical information and detailed historical and cultural background, with lots of practical travel information and detailed maps.

Iran, Lonely Planet Planet Guide
Constantly updated advice on what to see, what to eat, where to stay, as well as key cultural insights and advice.

MEDEA BENJAMIN

Culture Smart! Iran
Stuart Williams, 2016
A concise, well-illustrated and practical guide to local customs, etiquette, and culture.

ENDNOTES

INTRODUCTION

1 "Persia" was the official name of Iran in the Western world prior to 1935. Iranian and Persian are often used interchangeably but Persian relates to a particular ethnicity, while Iranian is a nationality. Modern Iran is comprised of a large number of different ethnic and tribal groups. People who identify as Persian account for the majority, but there are also Azeri, Galati, and Kurdish people. While all are citizens of Iran are Iranians, only some can identify their lineage as Persian.

2 https://www.vox.com/world/2017/9/21/16345600/bernie-sanders-full-text-transcript-foreign-policy-speech-westminster

CHAPTER 1

3 The main sources for the historical material in this chapter, supplemented as noted, are Michael Axworthy's *A History of Iran: Empire of the Mind*, New York, NY: Basic Books, 2008 and Ervand Abrahamian's *A History of Modern Iran*, New York, NY: Cambridge UP, 2008.

4 Durant, Will. "Persia in the History of Civilization," *Addressing 'Iran-America Society*. Mazda Publishers, Inc. July 23, 2011.

5 George Curzon, *Persia and the Persian Question*, p.136.

6 https://nvdatabase.swarthmore.edu/content/iranian-resistance-tobacco-concession-1891-1892

7 Kermit Roosevelt. *Countercoup: the Struggle for the Control of Iran*. New York, NY: McGraw-Hill, 1979. p. 6.

8 Brian Lapping. *End of Empire*. New York, NY: St. Martin's Press, 1985. pp. 204–223

9 https://partners.nytimes.com/library/world/mideast/082053iran-army.html

10   Frances FitzGerald, "Giving the Shah everything he wants." *Harper's*. November 1974.

11   Reza Baraheni, "Terror in Iran." *The New York Review of Books*. October 28 1976. http://www.nybooks.com/articles/1976/10/28/terror-in-iran/#fn-1

12   Ervand Abrahamian, *A History of Modern Iran*. New York, NY: Cambridge UP, 2008, p. 53.

CHAPTER 2

13   Ervand Abrahamian, *The Iranian Mojahedin*, Yale University Press, p121.

14   Roy Mottahedeh, *The Mantle of the Prophet: Religion and Politics in Iran,* 2004, p375.

15   Adam Roberts and Timothy Garton Ash, *Civil Resistance and Power Politics: The Experience of Non-violent Action*, Oxford University Press, 2009, p.51.

16   https://www.washingtonpost.com/archive/politics/1979/01/21/khomeini-from-oblivion-to-the-brink-of-powerlong-exile-from-iran-is-khomeinis-badge-and-handicap/02b4fc68-c0ae-4c71-b3ae-94ef68fefaae/?utm_term=.1013f5afb588

17   https://www.theguardian.com/politics/2012/sep/21/qanda-mek-us-terrorist-organisation

18   https://www.theguardian.com/world/2016/sep/09/iranian-opposition-groups-camp-ashraf-closes

19   https://www.amnesty.org/en/documents/MDE13/021/1990/en/

20   https://www.hrw.org/legacy/backgrounder/mena/iran1205/2.htm

21   https://www.niacouncil.org/kingmaker-irans-presidential-election/

CHAPTER 3

22   http://www.humanrights.com/what-are-human-rights/brief-history/

23   https://freedomhouse.org/report/freedom-world/2017/iran

24   http://www.thecrimson.com/article/1979/12/6/life-under-the-shah-pit-was/

25 https://freedomhouse.org/report/freedom-world/2017/iran
26 Ibid.
27 Situation of Human Rights in the Islamic Republic of Iran, UN
     Special Rapporteur on Human Rights, August 4, 2017.
28 https://berkleycenter.georgetown.edu/quotes/constitution-of-
     iran-article-26-freedom-of-association
29 https://www.ccij.ca/cases/kazemi/
30 Situation of Human Rights in the Islamic Republic of Iran, UN
     Special Rapporteur on Human Rights, August 4, 2017, p10.
31 http://www.li.com/docs/default-source/future-of-iran/2012-
     future-of-iran-by-karim-lahidji-the-history-of-the-judiciary-in-iran.
     pdf?sfvrsn=2
32 http://www.telegraph.co.uk/news/worldnews/middleeast/
     iran/8102358/Rape-in-Irans-prisons-the-cruellest-torture.html
33 https://www.amnesty.org/en/countries/middle-east-and-north-
     africa/iran/report-iran
34 Situation of Human Rights in the Islamic Republic of Iran, UN
     Special Rapporteur on Human Rights, August 4, 2017, p10.
35 http://www.ihrr.org/ihrr_article/violence-en_islamic-republic-of-
     iran-promoting-violence-against-children/
36 https://www.theguardian.com/artanddesign/gallery/2016/
     jan/08/inside-iran-jail-where-children-face-execution-in-pictures
37 http://www.iranhrdc.org/english/publications/human-rights-
     data/chart-of-prisoners/1000000595-chart-of-prisones.html
38 https://www.amnesty.org/en/countries/middle-east-and-north-
     africa/iran/report-iran
39 https://www.amnesty.org/en/latest/news/2012/03/iran-
     overturn-jail-sentence-human-rights-lawyer/
40 https://www.nytimes.com/2016/09/29/world/asia/narges-
     mohammadi-iran-sentencing.html?_r=0

CHAPTER 4

41 http://www.telegraph.co.uk/news/2017/10/04/us-votes-against-
     un-resolution-condemning-death-penalty-gay/
42 http://www.jpost.com/Middle-East/Iran-News/Iran-executes-gay-
     teenager-in-violation-of-international-law-463234

43 https://www.hrw.org/sites/default/files/reports/
iran1210webwcover_0.pdf
44 https://www.outrightinternational.org/region/islamic-republic-
iran
45 http://irqr.ca/2016/
46 https://www.theguardian.com/world/2005/jul/27/gayrights.iran
47 http://www.economist.com/node/2137652
48 https://www.theguardian.com/world/iran-blog/2014/oct/10/
iran-prostitution-sex-work-runaways
49 http://www.latimes.com/world/la-fg-iran-drug-addiction-2016-
story.html

CHAPTER 5

50 https://www.cia.gov/library/publications/the-world-factbook/
geos/ir.html (via Wikipedia)
51 https://www.theatlantic.com/international/archive/2016/01/
iran-sunnis-saudi/422877/
52 https://www.theatlantic.com/international/archive/2016/01/
iran-sunnis-saudi/422877/
53 http://www.mei.edu/content/article/iran%E2%80%99s-uneasy-
relationship-its-sunni-minorities
54 http://journal.georgetown.edu/iran-vs-its-people-abuses-against-
religious-minorities-by-katrina-lantos-swett/
55 https://www.al-monitor.com/pulse/originals/2017/09/iran-
tehran-sunni-mosque-prayer-space-pounak.html
56 https://freedomhouse.org/report/freedom-world/2017/iran
57 http://www.aljazeera.com/indepth/features/2014/03/iranian-
sunnis-complain-discrimination-2014397125688907.html
58 http://www.bbc.com/news/magazine-29648166
59 http://www.haaretz.com/middle-east-news/iran/1.813519
60 http://www.al-monitor.com/pulse/originals/2013/12/sufi-
practices-questioned-by-iranian-clerics.html
61 http://www.uscirf.gov/sites/default/files/USCIRF%202016%20
Annual%20Report.pdf
62 https://web.archive.org/web/20080422184053/http://www.fidh.
org/asie/rapport/2003/ir0108a.pdf

63 http://iranprimer.usip.org/blog/2016/jan/11/trends-parliamentary-elections

64 https://www.nytimes.com/2014/03/15/opinion/irans-oppressed-christians.html

65 http://www.uscirf.gov/youcef-nadarkhani

66 http://www.thenational.ae/news/world/middle-east/iran-is-young-urbanised-and-educated-census

67 https://www.jewishvirtuallibrary.org/jewish-population-of-the-world

68 Wright, *The Last Great Revolution*, (2000), p.207 (via Wikipedia)

69 https://www.timesofisrael.com/jewish-iranian-mp-lauds-countrys-religious-freedom/

70 http://www.independent.co.uk/news/world/middle-east/irans-jews-on-life-inside-israels-enemy-state-we-feel-secure-and-happy-a6934931.html

71 https://www.theguardian.com/world/2015/jun/01/first-christian-football-captain-in-iran-as-rouhani-puts-focus-on-minorities

72 http://www.uscirf.gov/sites/default/files/Iran.2017.pdf

73 http://www.bbc.com/news/world-middle-east-27438044

74 https://www.criticalthreats.org/briefs/iran-news-round-up/iran-news-round-up-may-16-2016-1

75 http://www.uscirf.gov/sites/default/files/Iran.2017.pdf

76 http://www.uscirf.gov/news-room/op-eds/the-wall-street-journal-whoever-wins-irans-election-its-religious-minorities-lose

77 http://www.uscirf.gov/news-room/op-eds/the-wall-street-journal-whoever-wins-irans-election-its-religious-minorities-lose

78 https://www.amnesty.org/en/countries/middle-east-and-north-africa/iran/report-iran/

79 https://www.iranhumanrights.org/2016/02/24-bahais-in-golestan-long-prison-sentences/

80 http://www.uscirf.gov/news-room/op-eds/the-wall-street-journal-whoever-wins-irans-election-its-religious-minorities-lose

81 http://www.uscirf.gov/sites/default/files/Iran.2017.pdf

82 http://www.loc.gov/law/help/apostasy/#iran

83 http://www.gallup.com/poll/114211/alabamians-iranians-common.aspx

CHAPTER 6

84 http://reports.weforum.org/global-gender-gap-report-2016/economies/#economy=IRN

85 https://www.amnesty.org/en/latest/news/2011/11/iranian-women-fight-controversial-polygamy-bill/

86 http://iranprimer.usip.org/resource/womens-movement

87 http://reports.weforum.org/global-gender-gap-report-2016/economies/#economy=IRN

88 http://www.latimes.com/world/la-fg-iran-unmarried-snap-story.html

89 http://www.atlanticcouncil.org/blogs/iraninsight/love-and-marriage-iranian-style

90 http://www.reuters.com/article/us-iran-divorce-idUSKCN0IB0GQ20141022

91 http://www.iranchamber.com/society/articles/abortion_iranian_law.php

92 DeJong, Jocelyn; Iman Mortagy; Bonnie Shepard (2005). "The Sexual and Reproductive Health of Young People in the Arab Countries and Iran." *Reproductive Health Matters*. **13** (25): 49–59.

93 http://iranprimer.usip.org/resource/womens-movement

94 https://euphrates.org/unveiling-and-reveiling-in-iran/

95 https://www.theguardian.com/world/2013/jul/02/iran-president-hassan-rouhani-progressive-views

96 http://www.nydailynews.com/life-style/makeup-speaks-volumes-iran-38-million-women-article-1.1841672

97 http://www.mei.edu/content/article/irans-headscarf-politics

98 http://www.bbc.com/news/world-middle-east-36101150

99 http://www.independent.co.uk/news/world/middle-east/iran-morality-police-14-year-old-girl-teenage-ripped-jeans-sharia-guidance-patrols-womens-right-a7582206.html

100 http://www.mei.edu/content/article/irans-headscarf-politics

101 http://www.bbc.com/news/world-middle-east-40218711

102 http://www.independent.co.uk/news/world/middle-east/lipstick-revolution-irans-women-are-taking-on-the-mullahs-1632257.html

103 Shavarini, Mitra K. (2005-01-01). "The Feminisation of Iranian Higher Education". International Review of Education /

Internationale Zeitschrift für Erziehungswissenschaft / Revue Internationale de l'Education. 51 (4): 329–347, 331, 333, 334, 335. JSTOR 25054545. (via Wikipedia)

104 http://wenr.wes.org/2017/02/education-in-iran

105 http://www.un.org/en/ga/search/view_doc. asp?symbol=A/70/352

106 Mehran, Golnar (2003-08-01). "The Paradox of Tradition and Modernity in Female Education in the Islamic Republic of Iran". Comparative Education Review. 47 (3): 269–286. ISSN 0010-4086. doi:10.1086/378248. (via Wikipedia)

107 Shavarini, Mitra K. (2005-01-01). "The Feminisation of Iranian Higher Education"

108 Mehran, Golnar (2003-08-01). "The Paradox of Tradition and Modernity in Female Education in the Islamic Republic of Iran".

109 Shavarini, Mitra K. (2005-01-01). "The Feminisation of Iranian Higher Education."

110 https://www.iranhumanrights.org/2015/02/womenreport-womens-education/

111 Povey, Tara; Rostami-Povey, Elaheh (2012). *Women, Power and Politics in 21st Century Iran*. Ashgate Publishing, Ltd. p. 42. ISBN 1409402053.

112 https://www.iranhumanrights.org/2015/02/womenreport-womens-education/

113 https://www.iranhumanrights.org/2015/02/womenreport-womens-education/

114 http://www.un.org/en/ga/search/view_doc. asp?symbol=A/70/352

115 https://www.hrw.org/report/2017/05/24/its-mens-club/discrimination-against-women-irans-job-market

116 https://www.hrw.org/report/2017/05/24/its-mens-club/discrimination-against-women-irans-job-market

117 https://www.iranhumanrights.org/2015/02/womenreport-womens-education/

118 https://www.usnews.com/news/best-countries/articles/2017-05-24/in-iran-women-want-rights-jobs-and-a-seat-at-the-table

119 https://www.hrw.org/report/2017/05/24/its-mens-club/
discrimination-against-women-irans-job-market
120 Ibid
121 Ibid
122 http://www.al-monitor.com/pulse/originals/2016/12/iran-
cabinet-reshuffle-women-vp-ministers-shojaei-ahmadipour.html
123 Ibid
124 http://indianexpress.com/article/world/iran-presidential-
elections-women-who-were-never-candidates-4661542/
125 http://www.bbc.com/news/world-middle-east-36182796
126 http://www.ipu.org/wmn-e/classif.htm
127 http://www.al-monitor.com/pulse/originals/2016/02/iran-
rouhani-women-vote-parliament-elections.html
128 https://www.rferl.org/a/iran-female-soccer-star-protests-
husband-travel-ban/27248135.html
129 https://www.nytimes.com/2016/07/03/sports/iranian-women-
push-for-more-open-stadiums.html?_r=0
130 https://www.nytimes.com/2016/07/03/sports/iranian-women-
push-for-more-open-stadiums.html?_r=0
131 https://www.amnesty.org/en/latest/news/2016/08/iran-
womens-rights-activists-treated-as-enemies-of-the-state-in-
renewed-crackdown/
132 https://www.usnews.com/news/best-countries/
articles/2017-05-24/in-iran-women-want-rights-jobs-and-a-seat-
at-the-table

CHAPTER 7

133 https://www.bloomberg.com/news/articles/2012-08-07/
goldman-sachs-s-mist-topping-brics-as-smaller-markets-
outperform
134 https://www.washingtonpost.com/archive/politics/1979/01/17/
pahlavi-fortune-a-staggering-sum/ef54b268-15c5-4ee5-b0a1-
194f90d87bba/?utm_term=.5f4b40f4560c
135 https://www.washingtonpost.com/archive/politics/1979/01/17/
pahlavi-fortune-a-staggering-sum/ef54b268-15c5-4ee5-b0a1-
194f90d87bba/?utm_term=.5f4b40f4560c

136 http://www.truth-out.org/news/item/22118-fruits-of-irans-revol ution?tmpl=component&print=1

137 Farhad Mumani and Sohrab Behdad. *Class and Labor in Iran: Did the Revolution Matter?*, Syracuse University Press, 2006, p 39.

138 http://www.ir.undp.org/content/iran/en/home/countryinfo. html

139 http://journal.georgetown.edu/the-ahmadinejad-presidency-and-the-future-of-irans-economy/

140 http://www.ft.com/content/4d017b7a-3cc2-11e3-86ef-00144feab7de?mhq5j=e1

141 http://www.ilo.org/dyn/natlex/docs/WEBTEXT/21843/64830/E90IRN01.htm

142 http://www.pbs.org/wgbh/pages/frontline/tehranbureau/2011/04/labors-struggle-for-independent-unions. html

143 https://www.equaltimes.org/iranian-workers-continue-to#. WawlvoqQw0o

144 Daniel Yergin, *The Prize: The Epic Quest for Oil, Money and Power.* Free Press, 2008, p.119.

145 https://en.wikipedia.org/wiki/Petroleum_industry_in_Iran#cite_note-15 (possibly sourced from *Kinzer, All the Shah's Men: An American Coup and the Roots of Middle East Terror* (John Wiley & Sons, 2003), p.166)

146 https://en.wikipedia.org/wiki/Petroleum_industry_in_Iran#cite_note-15 (Curtis, Glenn; Eric Hooglund. Iran, a country study (PDF). Washington D.C.: Library of Congress. pp. 160–163. ISBN 978-0-8444-1187-3)

147 http://oilprice.com/Energy/Crude-Oil/Iran-Plans-To-Raise-Crude-Oil-Production-Capacity-By-3-Million-Bpd.html

148 https://www.treasury.gov/resource-center/faqs/Sanctions/Pages/faq_iran.aspx

149 http://www.cnn.com/2012/01/23/world/meast/iran-sanctions-effects/index.html

150 Killing them Softly: The Start Impact of Sanctions on the Lives of Ordinary Iranians, International Civil Society Action Network, July 2012.

151 https://www.transparency.org/country/IRN

152 https://ajammc.com/2013/10/03/15-ways-sanctions-hurt-ordinary-iranians/

153 https://ajammc.com/2013/01/24/seeing-through-the-haze-the-politics-of-reporting-sanctions-and-smog-in-tehran/

154 http://www.newsmax.com/Newsfront/Iran-nuclear-deal-sanctions/2015/04/08/id/637354/

155 Parsi. *Losing an Enemy.* Pg 141

156 http://foreignpolicy.com/2014/05/14/no-sanctions-didnt-force-iran-to-make-a-deal/

157 https://www.bloomberg.com/news/articles/2017-04-06/leading-iranian-cleric-enters-election-in-threat-to-rouhani

158 http://www.reuters.com/article/us-peugeot-iran-idUSKCN10127V

CHAPTER 8

159 Slavin, Barbara. Bitter Friends, Bosom Enemies. Pg. 145–146

160 https://www.theguardian.com/world/iran-blog/2015/feb/11/us-general-huysers-secret-iran-mission-declassified

161 http://www.presidency.ucsb.edu/ws/?pid=7080

162 lombert. Negotiating. Pgs 99–101

163 http://www.nytimes.com/1992/01/26/world/us-secretly-gave-aid-to-iraq-early-in-its-war-against-iran.html?pagewanted=all

164 Slavin. *Bitter Friends.* Pg. 178

165 https://en.wikipedia.org/wiki/Iran%E2%80%93Contra_affair

166 http://www.nytimes.com/2001/09/21/world/a-nation-challenged-tehran-iran-softens-tone-against-the-united-states.html

167 http://www.pbs.org/wgbh/pages/frontline/showdown/themes/slapface.html

168 Parsi, Trita. Losing an Enemy. Pg. 43

169 Parsi. *Losing an Enemy.* Pg. 50

170 http://www.washingtonpost.com/wp-dyn/content/article/2009/03/20/AR2009032000398.html

171 Parsi. *Losing an Enemy.* Pg 85

172 Parsi, Trita. *A Single Roll of the Dice.* Pg. 183–84

173 Ibid. Pg. 161–73

174 http://thehill.com/homenews/administration/351323-trump-iran-nuclear-deal-an-embarrassment

175 http://foreignpolicy.com/2017/09/26/the-myth-of-a-better-iran-deal/

176 http://www.al-monitor.com/pulse/originals/2013/04/iranian-americans-human-rights-military.html

177 https://www.theguardian.com/commentisfree/2012/sep/23/iran-usa

178 https://www.theguardian.com/world/2012/sep/21/iran-mek-group-removed-us-terrorism-list

179 http://www.nytimes.com/2012/09/22/world/middleeast/iranian-opposition-group-mek-wins-removal-from-us-terrorist-list

CHAPTER 9

180 http://www.newsweek.com/surely-some-mistake-why-did-isis-attack-iran-625253

181 http://iranprimer.usip.org/resource/iran-and-israel

182 https://www.theguardian.com/world/2012/jan/11/secret-war-iran-timeline-attacks?intcmp=239

183 https://www.theglobeandmail.com/news/world/the-undeclared-war-on-irans-nuclear-program/article4210032/

184 http://www.jpost.com/Middle-East/Iran/Israel-behind-assassinations-of-Iran-nuclear-scientists-Yaalon-hints-411473#/

185 https://www.nytimes.com/2017/08/05/world/asia/iran-afghanistan-taliban.html

186 https://www.reuters.com/article/us-afghanistan-islamic-state/islamic-state-seizes-new-afghan-foothold-after-luring-taliban-defectors-idUSKBN1DV3G5

187 http://iranprimer.usip.org/resource/iran-and-turkey

188 https://www.al-monitor.com/pulse/originals/2015/09/iran-turkey-relations.html

189 https://www.huffingtonpost.com/entry/consequences-of-qatar-rapprochement-with-iran-and-turkey_us_59bab51ce4b02c642e4a1494

190 https://thediplomat.com/2017/07/iran-pakistan-at-the-crossroads/

191 https://www.foreignaffairs.com/articles/united-states/2013-01-15/tangle-caucasus

192 https://www.al-monitor.com/pulse/fr/originals/2015/11/iran-armenia-cooperation.html

193 https://thediplomat.com/2016/05/has-iran-finally-found-a-security-partner-in-central-asia/

194 https://www.pbs.org/newshour/world/iran-still-top-state-sponsor-terrorism-u-s-report-says

195 http://iranprimer.usip.org/resource/iran-and-israel

196 https://www.theatlantic.com/international/archive/2017/06/qatar-crisis-saudi-arabia-hamas-iran-syria-gcc-gaza/530229/

197 https://www.washingtonpost.com/news/monkey-cage/wp/2016/05/16/contrary-to-popular-belief-houthis-arent-iranian-proxies/?utm_term=.344ef5ce2449

198 https://www.theguardian.com/world/iran-blog/2016/apr/25/iran-russia-israel-tehranbureau

199 https://thediplomat.com/2016/01/chinas-relations-with-iran-a-threat-to-the-west/

200 http://iranprimer.usip.org/resource/iran-and-china

201 http://www.atlanticcouncil.org/blogs/iraninsight/the-u-s-is-pushing-iran-toward-china-2

202 http://www.mei.edu/content/map/japan-s-return-iran-risky-business

203 http://iranprimer.usip.org/blog/2016/may/23/south-korea-iran-boost-ties

204 https://newmatilda.com/2016/03/30/a-guide-to-australias-relationship-with-iran/

205 https://thediplomat.com/2016/07/the-reality-of-india-iran-ties/

206 https://www.bloomberg.com/news/features/2017-03-08/as-trump-makes-threats-iran-makes-friends

207 https://warisboring.com/irans-other-shadow-war-is-in-africa/

208 http://www.mepc.org/iran-horn-africa-outflanking-us-allies

209 https://reliefweb.int/report/eritrea/report-monitoring-group-somalia-and-eritrea-pursuant-security-council-resolution-2244

210 http://nationalinterest.org/feature/irans-awkward-diplomacy-africa-15571?page=2

CHAPTER 10

211 https://www.youtube.com/watch?v=o-zoPgv_nYg
212 https://www.huffingtonpost.com/ryan-costello/rep-sherman-favors-more-c_b_4352122.html
213 https://www.cnbc.com/2017/03/29/general-calls-iran-destabilizing-force-suggests-us-disrupt-regime-by-military-means.html
214 https://www.huffingtonpost.com/barry-lando/a-secret-war-against-iran_b_42218.html
215 Private conversation with Col. Wilkerson, October 22, 2017, Washington DC.
216 http://news.gallup.com/poll/116236/iran.aspx
217 http://www.politifact.com/truth-o-meter/statements/2015/apr/09/barack-obama/obama-iran-spends-30-billion-defense-us-about-600-/
218 https://en.wikipedia.org/wiki/List_of_countries_by_military_expenditures#List
219 http://www.politifact.com/truth-o-meter/statements/2015/apr/09/barack-obama/obama-iran-spends-30-billion-defense-us-about-600-/
220 https://www.theatlantic.com/magazine/archive/2016/04/the-obama-doctrine/471525/
221 http://www.newsweek.com/israel-and-egypt-pressured-obama-bomb-iran-nuclear-deal-725577

INDEX